olive

100 of the very best
ONE POT RECIPES

olive

100 of the very best ONE POT RECIPES

olive *magazine*

This edition first published in Great Britain in 2016 by Orion, an imprint of the Orion Publishing Group Ltd
Carmelite House
50 Victoria Embankment
London, EC4Y 0DZ
An Hachette UK Company

10 9 8 7 6 5 4 3 2 1

A CIP catalogue record for this book is available from the British Library.

ISBN: 978 1 4072 5 0632
Designed by Goldust Design
Printed in China

The Orion Publishing Group's policy is to use papers that are natural, renewable and recyclable and made from wood grown in sustainable forests. The logging and manufacturing processes are expected to conform to the environmental regulations of the country of origin.

www.orionbooks.co.uk

For more recipes visit olivemagazine.com

Contents

Introduction

olive is Britain's brightest food magazine. More than just a collection of recipes, it's about sharing the good stuff; cooking for family and friends, discovering great restaurants and enjoying weekends away. Upmarket and glossy, our recipe photography is the best in the market. In print and online at olivemagazine.com, we keep our audience up-to-date with new food trends and provide imaginative recipes for weeknights and weekends.

Quick one pot dishes are perfect for busy weeknights or for when you don't have time for unnecessary washing-up. In *100 of the Very Best One Pot Recipes*, we have put together a collection of our best recipes made in one dish, whether that's a pot, saucepan, tray or casserole. Some of the recipes will require an extra pot or saucepan for sides, or a bowl for mixing or measuring, but we have tried to keep any additional equipment to a minimum. Every recipe includes our trademark photography, so you know exactly what you are aiming for. From cheat's seafood stew, quick chicken jalfrezi to smoky baked pork and beans and fig tarte tatins, this is the only collection of one pot recipes you will need.

At **olive**, we believe you can eat well at home even if you don't have bags of time. Most of the recipes in this book are quick and easy, and can be made using easily accessible ingredients and equipment found in your kitchen. We think weekends are for more adventurous cooking so we have also included some recipes that will take more time, but will be oh so worth it.

Notes and conversion tables

There are three categories of recipes throughout the *olive* books.

Easy: Most of our recipes come under this category and are very simple to put together with easy-to-find ingredients.

A little effort: These recipes require either more time, shopping for harder to find ingredients or a little more complicated cooking techniques.

Tricky but worth it: We have offered a few recipes that fall under this category and require a higher level of skill and concentration. These recipes give readers an occasional challenge, but the little extra effort is always well worth the reward.

- Recipe timings are based on the total amount of time needed to finish the recipe so includes both prep and cook time.
- Provenance matters to us. Where possible, we use free-range eggs and chickens, humanely reared meat, organic dairy products, sustainably caught fish, unrefined sugar and fairly traded ingredients.
- Nutritional information is provided for all recipes. Because *olive* recipes don't always give exact quantities for ingredients such as oil and butter, nutritional quantities may not always be 100 per cent accurate. Analysis includes only the listed ingredients, not optional ingredients, such as salt, or any serving suggestions.
- Care should be taken when buying meat that you intend to eat raw or rare.
- Our recipes use large eggs, unless otherwise stated. Pregnant women, the elderly, babies and toddlers, and people who are unwell should avoid eating raw and partially cooked eggs.
- Vegetarians should always check the labels on shop-bought ingredients such as yoghurt, cheese, pesto and curry sauces, to ensure they are suitable for vegetarian consumption.
- Unless otherwise specified, if oil is listed as an ingredient, any flavourless oil such as groundnut, vegetable or sunflower oil can be used.

Liquid measurements

Metric	Imperial	Australian	US
25ml	1fl oz		
60ml	2fl oz	¼ cup	¼ cup
75ml	3fl oz		
100ml	3½fl oz		
120ml	4fl oz	½ cup	½ cup
150ml	5fl oz		
180ml	6fl oz	¾ cup	¾ cup
200ml	7fl oz		
250ml	9fl oz	1 cup	1 cup
300ml	10½fl oz	1¼ cups	1¼ cups
350ml	12½fl oz	1½ cups	1½ cups
400ml	14fl oz	1¾ cups	1¾ cups
450ml	16fl oz	2 cups	2 cups
600ml	1 pint	2½ cups	2½ cups
750ml	1¼ pints	3 cups	3 cups
900ml	1½ pints	3½ cups	3½ cups
1 litre	1¾ pints	1 quart or 4 cups	1 quart or 4 cups
1.2 litres	2 pints		
1.4 litres	2½ pints		
1.5 litres	2¾ pints		
1.7 litres	3 pints		
2 litres	3½ pints		

Oven temperature guide

	Electricity			Gas
	°C	°F	(Fan) °C	Mark
Very cool	110	225	90	¼
	120	250	100	½
Cool	140	275	120	1
	150	300	130	2
Moderate	160	325	140	3
	170	350	150	4
Moderately hot	190	375	170	5
	200	400	180	6
Hot	220	425	200	7
	230	450	210	8
Very hot	240	475	220	9

Meat-free

Fiery chickpea and harissa soup

30 minutes | serves 4 | easy

1 onion, chopped
1 tbsp olive oil
2 carrots, peeled and diced
2 celery sticks, diced
½ tsp ground cumin
2 tbsp harissa
400g can chickpeas,
    drained and rinsed
750ml vegetable stock
2 tbsp tomato purée
handful of parsley leaves,
    chopped, to serve
salt and freshly ground
    black pepper

A fast-to-make and easy spicy soup made with chickpeas. This vegetarian recipe gets its heat from harissa, a hot chilli pepper paste from Morocco.

Cook the onion in the oil in a pan until softened. Add the carrots and celery and cook for 5 minutes. Stir in the cumin and harissa and cook for 1 minute. Add the rest of the ingredients except the parsley, season, then bring to a simmer. Cook for 15 minutes then stir in the parsley before serving.

Per serving 188 kcals, **protein** 6.8g, **carbohydrate** 23.1g, **fat** 5.7g, **saturated fat** 0.7g, **fibre** 8.6g, **salt** 1g

Tortellini in a pea broth

10 minutes | serves 2 | easy

500ml vegetable stock
250g pack tortellini
2 handfuls of frozen peas, defrosted
½ small bunch of basil leaves, shredded
½ lemon
grated Parmesan and crusty bread, to serve (optional)
salt and freshly ground black pepper

This simple, stylish-looking tortellini in a pea broth is super quick and delicious, too. It's everything you want from a midweek one pot supper – ready in just 10 minutes.

Heat the stock in a pan. Add the tortellini and cook until just tender, adding the peas for the last 2 minutes of cooking. Season then stir in the basil. Add a squeeze of the lemon.

Spoon into bowls and serve with crusty bread and a sprinkling of grated Parmesan, if you like.

Per serving 398 kcals, **protein** 15g, **carbohydrate** 62.3g, **fat** 11.6g, **saturated fat** 5.4g, **fibre** 3.4g, **salt** 3.18g

Cauliflower and cannellini bean soup

25 minutes | serves 4 | easy

1 small/medium
 cauliflower (about 500g)
25g butter
750ml chicken stock
sprig of rosemary
1 tbsp sea salt flakes
410g can cannellini beans,
 drained and rinsed
4 tbsp double cream
olive oil, to serve
freshly ground black
 pepper

Creamy cauliflower and cannellini bean soup is sprinkled with rosemary sea salt, ground black pepper and a drizzle of olive oil. Serve with crusty bread for a warming lunch or supper.

Cut the cauliflower into small florets – you should end up with around 450g after trimming. Put the florets in a pan with the butter and cook it gently for about 5 minutes. Pour over the chicken stock. Cover and bring to a simmer, then cook for 12–15 minutes or until very tender – don't be tempted to add extra water or the finished soup will be too thin.

Remove the leaves from the rosemary and put them in a pile on a board with the salt. Chop the salt and rosemary together until very, very fine. Set aside.

Blitz the soup with a stick blender until smooth then stir in the cannellini beans and double cream. Warm through gently, then season to taste with a touch of salt and some pepper – be careful with the salt, as more will be added with the rosemary. Ladle into warmed soup bowls. Sprinkle with the rosemary and salt mixture, adding a grind of pepper and drizzle of olive oil.

Per serving 280 kcals, **protein** 10.7g, **carbohydrate** 15.9g, **fat** 19.8g, **saturated fat** 8.9g, **fibre** 5.7g, **salt** 3.84g

Thai carrot and lemongrass soup

30 minutes | serves 2 | easy

1 tbsp oil

1 onion, roughly chopped

1 garlic clove, roughly
  chopped

1 lemongrass stalk,
  woody outer leaves
  removed and tender core
  chopped

chunk of fresh root ginger,
  peeled and grated

500g carrots, peeled
  and chopped

165ml can coconut milk

600ml vegetable stock

grated zest and juice
  of 1 lime

Thai cuisine uses fragrant flavours to create warming and comforting dishes. Our Thai carrot and lemongrass soup is an easy vegetarian option, with plenty of zing from the lemongrass and ginger, plus the coconut milk makes the soup really creamy.

Heat the oil in a pan and cook the onion, garlic, lemongrass and ginger for 5 minutes. Add the carrots and cook for another 5 minutes. Stir the coconut milk in its can in case it has separated then take out 2 tablespoons and set aside to finish the soup. Add the rest of the milk to the carrots with the stock. Simmer until the carrots are tender then whizz with a stick blender until smooth.

Stir in the lime juice and zest then spoon into bowls and drizzle over the reserved coconut milk to finish.

Per serving 197 kcals, **protein** 3.5g, **carbohydrate** 30.8g, **fat** 7g, **saturated fat** 1.5g, **fibre** 8.6g, **salt** 0.4g

Smoky sweet potato soup

30 minutes | serves 4 | easy

knob of butter
1 onion, roughly chopped
1 tsp hot smoked paprika,
    plus extra to serve
1 tsp ground coriander
2 garlic cloves, crushed
750g sweet potatoes,
    peeled and cut into
    chunks
1 litre vegetable stock
75g Gruyère (or vegetarian
    alternative), grated
salt and freshly ground
    black pepper

This smoky sweet potato soup is a quick and easy winter warmer. Make a batch for the family or eat some now and freeze the rest for later.

Melt the butter in a large pan, add the onion, paprika, coriander and garlic and cook for about 8 minutes until softened. Add the sweet potato and cook for a few more minutes. Add the stock, bring to the boil then simmer, covered, for 10 minutes, or until the veg is soft.

Whizz in a blender or with a stick blender to a smooth soup. Season and serve with a sprinkling of grated cheese and an extra pinch of paprika, if you like.

Per serving 298 kcals, **protein** 8.8g, **carbohydrate** 42.5g, **fat** 8.6g, **saturated fat** 4.8g, **fibre** 7.8g, **salt** 1.1g

Spring broth

15 minutes | serves 4 | easy

1 large onion,
    finely chopped
1 garlic clove, crushed
olive oil, for frying
500g spring cabbage,
    finely shredded
1.5 litres vegetable stock
small bunch of parsley,
    chopped
100g feta, crumbled
salt and freshly ground
    black pepper

A comforting soup bursting with the flavours of spring – cabbage, garlic, onion – and topped with feta. Spring cabbages such as Primo make a good base for fresher-flavoured ingredients such as feta.

Fry the onion and garlic in olive oil in a large saucepan until soft but not coloured – this will take about 5 minutes. Add the cabbage, stock and parsley and bring to a simmer, then cook for 5 minutes or until the cabbage is soft. Season well. Serve in deep bowls with the feta stirred through.

Per serving 280 kcals, **protein** 21.3g, **carbohydrate** 11.8g, **fat** 16.9g, **saturated fat** 4.3g, **fibre** 4.1g, **salt** 0.25g

Tuscan bean and barley stew

30 minutes | serves 4 | easy

2 tbsp olive oil
1 garlic clove, crushed
2 carrots, diced small
2 celery sticks, peeled and
  diced small
1 large leek, finely
  chopped
900ml vegetable stock
1 tbsp tomato purée
3 tbsp pearl barley
400g can borlotti beans,
  drained and rinsed
about 150g leafy greens,
  woody stalks removed,
  leaves shredded
crusty bread, to serve

This stew is perfect to have on hand for a quick and warming supper. You can use any leafy greens for this, just add in whatever you have around.

Heat the oil in a large pan then add the garlic, carrots, celery and leek and cook until softened. Add the stock, tomato purée and barley. Bring to a simmer then cook for 15–20 minutes until the barley is just tender. Add the beans and greens and simmer for 5 more minutes. Serve with crusty bread.

Per serving 196 kcals, **protein** 7.6g, **carbohydrate** 25.5g, **fat** 7.8g, **saturated fat** 0.8g, **fibre** 6.5g, **salt** 2.68g

Creamed corn with chilli and smoky paprika

40 minutes | serves 4 or 6 as a side | easy

4 large corn cobs, husks
    removed and kernels
    cut off
2 onions, finely chopped
1 garlic clove, crushed
1 red chilli, deseeded and
    finely chopped
25g butter
1 tbsp rapeseed oil
½ tsp smoked paprika
250ml double cream
200ml water
coriander leaves, to serve
salt and freshly ground
    black pepper

A simple side that uses fresh corn on the cob. Chilli gives it a kick of heat. This is great as part of a vegetarian meal, or if you do eat meat, it goes well with grilled chicken or fish.

Put the corn kernels, onions, garlic and chilli in a pan (with a lid), with the butter and oil and cook over a very low heat for about 10 minutes, or until the onion is translucent and the corn is soft but not browning. Stir in the paprika for 1 minute to toast.

Add the cream with the water, then bring to a gentle simmer before covering and cooking for 10 minutes.

Lift off the lid and, using a stick blender, blitz roughly half of the corn in the pan. Bubble gently without the lid for about another 10 minutes or until the corn is thick and creamy. Season well, particularly with salt, and scatter with coriander leaves to serve.

Per serving (4) 356 kcals, **protein** 4.2g, **carbohydrate** 17.9g, **fat** 29.2g, **saturated fat** 16.4g, **fibre** 2.6g, **salt** 0.5g

Baked mushroom, potato and cheese hash with eggs

50 minutes | serves 2 | easy

500g floury potatoes,
   diced into 1cm chunks
100–150g wild or mixed
   mushrooms, halved
   if large
1 tbsp olive oil
1 tbsp butter, melted, plus
   a knob extra for greasing
1 tbsp grainy mustard
50g Gruyère, grated,
   plus a little extra
2 tbsp chives, snipped
2 eggs
salt and freshly ground
   black pepper

Midweek potatoes made even better. Mashed potatoes mixed with Gruyère cheese and mustardy mushrooms baked in the oven and finished off with an egg on top – all ready in under an hour.

Boil the potatoes in a big pan of salted water until almost tender. Drain well, then tip back into the pan, cover with a lid and allow to steam dry off the heat for a few minutes.

Preheat the oven to 220°C/Fan 200°C/Gas 7. Tip the mushrooms, olive oil, melted butter, mustard, cheese and most of the chives into the potato pan with plenty of seasoning and mix everything together well. Grease a small baking tray/tin or small individual dishes with a little more butter, then tip in the potatoes and mushrooms. Squash down to flatten and crush together. Make 2 dips in the mixture (you'll be cracking the eggs into these later).

Scatter a little more cheese over the top and bake for 25–30 minutes until golden.

Crack the eggs into the dips and bake for another 5–8 minutes until cooked to your liking. Sprinkle over the remaining chives to serve.

Per serving 543 kcals, **protein** 21.2g, **carbohydrate** 42.1g, **fat** 31g, **saturated fat** 13.1g, **fibre** 5.7g, **salt** 1.7g

Spring onion and roasted red pepper frittata

30 minutes | serves 2 | easy

½ bunch of spring onions, chopped (including green bits)

knob of butter, for cooking

2 large roasted red peppers from a jar, drained and chopped

300g large cooked new potatoes, peeled and sliced

6 eggs, beaten

salad, to serve

salt and freshly ground black pepper

Frittata is an Italian-style omelette. This one, with its peppers, spring onions and new potatoes, is a quick and easy meal for two. All it needs is salad on the side. This is good served cold for lunch the next day, too – if there are any leftovers.

Cook the spring onions in a large knob of butter in a frying pan until soft. Mix into the eggs with the peppers and potatoes and season well.

Preheat the grill. Heat a small 20cm non-stick pan with a little butter then tip in the egg mix. Cook gently until the bottom is set, then slide the pan under the grill until the top is golden and just set. Serve with salad.

Per serving 400 kcals, **protein** 22.8g, **carbohydrate** 29.8g, **fat** 21.8g, **saturated fat** 7.6g, **fibre** 2.8g, **salt** 0.8g

Roast new potatoes with taleggio and capers

35 minutes | serves 6 | easy

1kg small new potatoes,
   scrubbed clean
olive oil, for coating
200g taleggio, rind cut
   off and cheese sliced
2 tbsp capers, rinsed
   and drained
4 spring onions, chopped
splash of red wine vinegar
salt and freshly ground
   black pepper

Inspired by a cheesy, dripping, roast potato side dish, we decided to make our own version. Indulgent – but so good.

Preheat the oven to 200°C/Fan 180°C/Gas 6. Toss the potatoes in olive oil and lots of seasoning. Spread the potatoes out on a non-stick baking tray or casserole. Roast for 25–30 minutes until golden and tender. Lay over the cheese slices, then put back in the oven for a few minutes until the cheese is just melted.

Mix the capers and spring onions with a splash of red wine vinegar and olive oil and season. Spoon this over the potatoes before serving.

Per serving 252 kcals, **protein** 9.1g, **carbohydrate** 25.8g, **fat** 12.6g, **saturated fat** 6.2g, **fibre** 2.4g, **salt** 1.3g

Little Gem lettuce and Parmesan risotto

30 minutes | serves 4 | easy

knob of butter, for frying
1 onion, finely chopped
2 garlic cloves,
   finely chopped
350g carnaroli or Arborio
   risotto rice
1 large glass of dry white
   wine
1.5 litres hot fresh
   vegetable stock, or made
   from a cube or
   concentrate
50g Parmesan or Grana
   Padano, grated, plus extra
   to serve (optional)
2 Little Gem lettuces,
   torn into small pieces
salt and freshly ground
   black pepper

This is a quick and easy risotto for when you need something comforting, fast. Try adding a couple of bay leaves with the wine and then some peas in the last few minutes for an extra twist.

Melt the butter in a large pan, add the onion and garlic and cook until soft and translucent. Stir in the rice until coated with the butter. Add the white wine and cook, stirring, until evaporated. Add the stock a ladle at a time, until the rice is cooked but still has a little bite (you might not need to use all the stock).

Season and stir through the cheese and the lettuce to gently wilt the leaves. Serve with extra cheese, if you like.

Per serving 431 kcals, **protein** 13.7g, **carbohydrate** 76.9g, **fat** 8.1g, **saturated fat** 4.4g, **fibre** 6.1g, **salt** 4.1g

Roasted roots and goat's cheese

50 minutes | serves 2 | easy

2 raw beetroots, peeled
and sliced

5 baby carrots, halved
lengthways

2 small parsnips, peeled
and sliced lengthways
a little thicker than the
beetroot

1 red onion, sliced into
thick discs

2 individual goat's cheese
with rind (90–100g each),
to serve

handful of rocket leaves,
to serve

crusty bread or warm Puy
lentils, to serve

salt and freshly ground
black pepper

For the dressing

3 tbsp red wine vinegar

1 tbsp olive oil

1 tbsp clear honey

1 red chilli, deseeded
and diced

grated zest and juice
of ½ orange

Think carrots are boring? This fast and fresh recipe roasts the roots with cumin, chilli and mustard seeds until caramelised and sweet, then finishes with fresh coriander and goat's cheese. Serve as a side dish or as a vegetarian main with couscous.

Preheat the oven to 190°C/Fan 170°C/Gas 5. Mix all the dressing ingredients with some freshly ground black pepper and salt. Reserve 1 tablespoon of the dressing for later.

Pile the sliced beetroots, carrots, parsnips and onion into a baking dish or individual potions. Drizzle over the rest of the dressing, then toss together so everything is well coated. Roast for 30–35 minutes, until all the veg is almost tender.

Sit a goat's cheese on top of the pile of veg. Put back in the oven for 3–5 minutes, until the cheese feels soft and hot to the touch. Spoon over the reserved dressing and serve with rocket leaves, crusty bread or some warm Puy lentils.

Per serving 390 kcals, **protein** 14.6g, **carbohydrate** 33.6g, **fat** 19.8g, **saturated fat** 9.9g, **fibre** 9.6g, **salt** 1g

Pesto, pea and bean risotto

25 minutes | serves 4 | easy

200g mixture of peas,
   broad beans and green
   beans, cut into short
   lengths
800ml vegetable stock,
   at simmering point
butter, for cooking
olive oil, for cooking
1 onion, finely chopped
300g carnaroli risotto rice
100ml white wine
2-3 tbsp pesto
handful of basil leaves
grated Parmesan, to serve
salt and freshly ground
   black pepper

This risotto is quick to make and requires few ingredients. It makes a lovely, vibrant-looking, speedy supper or lunch.

Blanch the veg in the simmering stock for 3-4 minutes in a wide, shallow pan then remove with a slotted spoon, transfer to a bowl and add a small knob of butter. Pour the stock into a heatproof measuring jug and set aside.

Melt a knob of butter with a dash of olive oil in the same pan and add the onion. Cook until softened, but don't let it brown. Tip in the rice and stir for 1 minute until it starts to look translucent. Add the wine and stir until it evaporates. Pour in enough stock to just cover the rice and gently simmer, stirring now and again. As the stock evaporates and the rice swells, add more stock and stir intermittently until all the stock is used or until the rice is just tender – this will take 15-17 minutes.

Once the rice is cooked but still retains a hint of bite, beat in a knob of butter until the risotto is creamy, then stir in the pesto. Season.

Reheat the veg if you need to, then spoon it over the risotto and finish with a scattering of basil leaves and Parmesan.

Per serving 414 kcals, **protein** 10.5g, **carbohydrate** 67.1g, **fat** 12.5g, **saturated fat** 4.7g, **fibre** 4g, **salt** 2.27g

Chickpea and tomato tagine

30 minutes | serves 2 | easy

olive oil, for cooking

½ tsp ground cumin

½ tsp paprika

½ tsp ground ginger

1 Spanish onion,
   roughly chopped

1 red pepper, deseeded
   and cut into cubes

250g pumpkin, peeled,
   deseeded and cut
   into cubes

250ml water

pinch of saffron (optional)

5 tomatoes, roughly
   chopped

400g can chopped
   tomatoes

400g can chickpeas,
   drained and rinsed

salt and freshly ground
   black pepper

A tagine doesn't need to simmer for hours to taste delicious. This veggie version is ready in just 30 minutes and is full of flavour.

Heat a little oil in a large saucepan or casserole and stir in the cumin, paprika and ginger. Add the vegetables and fry for 5 minutes, keeping them moving so they brown evenly. Add the water, the saffron (if using), tomatoes and some seasoning, then bring to a simmer. Cover and cook for 10 minutes, then stir in the chickpeas and cook, uncovered, for a further 10 minutes until the veg is tender.

Per serving 294 kcals, **protein** 13.2g, **carbohydrate** 42.2g, **fat** 9.2g, **saturated fat** 0.7g, **fibre** 1.2g, **salt** 0.08g

Bombay egg and potato curry

40 minutes | serves 2 | easy

2 onions, 1 chopped,
   1 quartered
1 tbsp sunflower oil
2 green chillies,
   1 halved and deseeded,
   1 finely sliced
2 garlic cloves
handful of coriander,
   leaves and stalks
   separated
2 tsp each turmeric,
   garam masala, ground
   cumin, fennel and black
   mustard seeds
1 vegetable stock cube
400g can chopped
   tomatoes
150ml coconut milk
400g potatoes, peeled and
   cut into 2.5cm cubes
3 eggs
juice of 1 lemon
basmati rice or warm
   chapatis, to serve
salt and freshly ground
   black pepper

Some nights you don't want to have to spend ages shopping to make a delicious meal. This Bombay egg and potato curry can be made using storecupboard ingredients and is ready in just 40 minutes. You will need to boil the eggs in an extra pot, but everything else is cooked in just one pan.

Fry the chopped onions in the oil in a large frying pan or shallow casserole until soft and golden.

Meanwhile, whizz the quartered onion, halved chilli, garlic and coriander stalks with ¼ teaspoon of salt to a paste in a small blender – add a splash of water to loosen if necessary.

Once the onions are soft, stir in the paste and spices and fry for 4–5 minutes until fragrant. Crumble in the stock cube, stir in the tomatoes and coconut milk with a can of water and bring to a simmer. Add the potatoes, cover with a lid and simmer for 8 minutes.

Meanwhile, gently lower the whole eggs into a pan of boiling water and cook for 8 minutes. Cool in cold water then peel and quarter the cooked eggs.

Take the lid off the curry and let it carry on bubbling for 10–15 minutes until the potatoes are tender and the sauce has reduced and thickened. Taste the curry and season with more salt, black pepper and lemon juice. Snuggle the eggs in, turn off the heat and sit the lid back on top so the eggs warm up for a minute or so.

To serve, scatter with the sliced green chilli and the coriander leaves and eat with basmati rice or warm chapatis.

Per serving 601 kcals, **protein** 21.1g, **carbohydrate** 55.4g, **fat** 30.8g, **saturated fat** 14.5g, **fibre** 8.7g, **salt** 2g

Tomato and onion bake

2 hours 15 minutes | serves 6 | easy

150g butter
1.5kg onions, thinly sliced
1.5kg tomatoes, a mix of
    any type you like
    (a variety works best)
    very ripe, cut into 1cm
    thick slices
100g fresh breadcrumbs
salt and freshly ground
    black pepper

This easy bake requires few ingredients, little hands-on time and needs minimal washing up! It does take a little longer, but it is easy to put in the oven and not think about.

Grease a large ovenproof dish with some of the butter. Fry the onions gently with a knob of the butter in a pan over a low heat until soft.

Preheat the oven to 200°C/Fan 180°C/Gas 6. Layer the vegetables in the dish: onions first, then the tomatoes – a few overlapping – then season and add a few knobs of butter, then the next layer. As you layer, the dish should become overfull and look like a mountain – as it cooks the whole lot will soften and drop.

Cover with the breadcrumbs and a few more knobs of the butter and put in the oven. Once in, turn the oven down to 180°C/Fan 160°C/Gas 4 and cook for 1¼ hours.

Serve hot, or cold – or sneak it from the fridge in big mouthfuls when no one is watching.

Per serving 378 kcals, **protein** 6.8g, **carbohydrate** 37.7g, **fat** 22.1g, **saturated fat** 13.3g, **fibre** 6.4g, **salt** 0.8g

Cauliflower, fennel and herb risotto

40 minutes | serves 4 | easy

knob of butter

1 onion, finely chopped

1 garlic clove, finely
chopped

½ small head cauliflower,
roughly chopped

1 fennel bulb, halved
and shredded

300g Arborio risotto rice

125ml white wine

1 litre hot vegetable stock

1 tbsp chopped parsley

salt and freshly ground
black pepper

Risotto is a sure-fire winner for an easy meal. Arborio risotto rice is a great all-rounder. It will give a creamy finished dish with that classic soupiness that we all crave from a risotto. Cauliflower and fennel are cooked in the pan so that all their delicious flavours soak into the rice. Finish with butter and fresh chopped parsley.

Melt a little of the butter in a wide, shallow pan then cook the onion and garlic until softened. Add the cauliflower and fennel and cook for 2–3 minutes. Add the rice and turn to coat in the butter. Tip in the wine and stir until absorbed.

Gradually add the stock, stirring for about 15 minutes, or until you have a creamy risotto with a little bite. Stir in the parsley with another knob of butter and season.

Per serving 335 kcals, **protein** 9g, **carbohydrate** 67g, **fat** 4g, **saturated fat** 1g, **fibre** 4g, **salt** 2.63g

Steakhouse-style spinach gratin

1 hour 10 minutes | serves 6 as a side | easy

1kg spinach leaves,
   washed, stems removed
   and leaves chopped
50g butter
4 tbsp plain flour
250ml double cream
2 shallots, finely chopped
150g Cheddar, grated
2 tbsp dried breadcrumbs
large pinch of paprika

This is a different way to eat spinach and a great way to get one of your five-a-day. A typical side in most steakhouses, this easy gratin recipe makes the perfect accompaniment for a supper with friends.

Heat a very large pan or wide casserole, then tip in the spinach with a splash of water. Stir until completely wilted, transfer to a colander to cool, then squeeze out all the excess water (a clean tea towel is good for this).

Preheat the oven to 190°C/Fan 170°C/Gas 5. Melt the butter in the pan, stir in the flour and cook for 2 minutes. Whisk in the cream, then simmer for a couple of minutes until the mixture thickens. Add the shallots, spinach and most of the grated Cheddar.

Spoon into the wide casserole or 6 individual ovenproof dishes. Mix the breadcrumbs, remaining cheese and paprika together then sprinkle it over the top. Bake in the oven for 40 minutes or until golden, or 25 minutes for the individual dishes.

Per serving 478 kcals, **protein** 13.6g, **carbohydrate** 16.6g, **fat** 40g, **saturated fat** 24g, **fibre** 5.4g, **salt** 1.3g

Pan haggerty

50 minutes | serves 4 | easy

2 tbsp vegetable oil
2 onions, thinly sliced
2 tbsp goose fat, lard or
    more oil, melted
800g floury potatoes
    (such as King Edward),
    peeled and thinly sliced
a couple of handfuls of
    grated Cheddar cheese
salt and freshly ground
    black pepper

Hailing from Northumberland, pan haggerty combines layers of buttery potato and onion topped with bubbling Cheddar cheese. This one pot dish is sure to warm your bones. Serve with steamed winter greens on the side.

Preheat the oven to 200°C/Fan 180°C/Gas 6. Heat the oil in an ovenproof frying pan and soften the onions for 7 minutes until they start to caramelise. Remove and drain on kitchen paper. Clean the pan, return to the heat and add half the fat.

Add a layer of potato, then onion and season. Repeat until you have used all the potatoes and onions. Spoon over the remaining melted fat, cover with foil and cook on a high shelf in the oven for 25–30 minutes. Remove the foil and test with a sharp knife – it should glide through easily.

Sprinkle with the Cheddar then pop under a hot grill until golden and bubbly. Run a knife around the edges and slide onto a plate or serve straight from the pan.

Per serving 369 kcals, **protein** 7.3g, **carbohydrate** 22.2g, **fat** 21.5g, **saturated fat** 7.7g, **fibre** 2.2g, **salt** 0.34g

Winter greens and ricotta cannelloni

1½ hours | serves 8 | a little effort

knob of butter

olive oil

1 large onion, diced

2 garlic cloves, crushed

2 sprigs of thyme, leaves
   picked

glass of white wine

250g ricotta

good grating of nutmeg

400g winter greens
   (we used cavolo nero
   and kale), tough stalks
   removed and leaves
   chopped

200g dried cannelloni
   tubes

2 x 400g cans chopped
   tomatoes

1 bay leaf

250g mascarpone

50g Parmesan, Grana
   Padano (or veggie
   alternative), grated

salt and freshly ground
   black pepper

This winter greens and ricotta cannelloni is a great vegetarian main to store in your freezer. The recipe is easily doubled, so why not make one and freeze another for later?

Heat the butter and a drizzle of olive oil in a large frying pan. Fry the onion until softened, then add half the garlic and all the thyme. Fry for another minute, then stir in the wine. Simmer until reduced by half, then add the ricotta and nutmeg and season. Stir in the greens and cook until wilted, adding a splash of water if you need to. Leave to cool a little.

Preheat the oven to 180°C/Fan 160°C/Gas 4. Using a teaspoon, fill the cannelloni tubes with the mixture, and put the tubes in a single layer in an ovenproof dish.

In the same frying pan used to make the ricotta mixture, fry the remaining garlic in 1 tablespoon of oil for a minute, then add the chopped tomatoes and the bay leaf. Simmer for 10 minutes until the tomatoes have broken down, then add a splash of water to make a sauce. Season and spoon over the cannelloni tubes, covering them completely.

Mix the mascarpone with the Parmesan and season. Dollop over the top of the cannelloni, then bake for 30–35 minutes until golden and bubbling. Eat now, or allow to cool completely, cover with foil and freeze. To reheat, defrost in the fridge overnight then bake again for 20–30 minutes until piping hot in the centre.

Per serving 380 kcals, **protein** 13.4g, **carbohydrate** 28.9g, **fat** 21.9g, **saturated fat** 14.2g, **fibre** 2.2g, **salt** 0.4g

Chicken, poultry and game

Smoky chicken and bean stew

30 minutes | serves 2 | easy

1 small red onion, sliced

2 garlic cloves, crushed

1 tbsp olive oil

1 tbsp mild chilli powder

½ red pepper, deseeded
   and cut into chunks

4 skinless chicken thigh
   fillets, cut into strips

40g pack sliced chorizo,
   cut into strips

4 tomatoes, chopped

300ml chicken stock

400g can borlotti beans,
   drained and rinsed

½ small bunch of coriander,
   chopped

wholemeal pitta bread,
   to serve

salt and freshly ground
   black pepper

This smoky chicken and bean stew with chorizo and a chilli kick is hearty and delicious. You just need one pot and it's on the table in 30 minutes – perfect for a hassle-free midweek meal.

Cook the onion and garlic in the oil until softened. Add the chilli powder and pepper and cook for 1 minute. Add the chicken and chorizo and fry for a couple of minutes. Stir in the tomatoes and stock and bring to a simmer. Add the beans and cook for 15–20 minutes until thickened.

Stir in the coriander, season and serve in bowls with the pitta bread.

Per serving 529 kcals, **protein** 58g, **carbohydrate** 34.1g, **fat** 18.8g, **saturated fat** 4.8g, **fibre** 8.4g, **salt** 2.25g

Middle Eastern chicken and apricot stew

30 minutes | serves 4 | easy

1 tbsp olive oil

1 large onion, chopped

1 tbsp grated fresh root
  ginger

2 garlic cloves, chopped

4 skinless chicken breasts,
  cut into chunks

2 tsp baharat or ras el
  hanout spice blend

100g red lentils

10 ready-to-eat apricots,
  finely chopped

juice of 1 lemon

750ml chicken stock
  or water

handful each of mint and
  coriander, or a mix of
  both, chopped

handful of pomegranate
  seeds (optional)

rice or couscous, to serve

salt and freshly ground
  black pepper

**This stew is full of spicy Middle Eastern flavours. Serve with a side
of rice or couscous to soak up all of the lovely juices.**

Heat the olive oil in a pan. Add the onion, ginger and garlic and season.
Cook for 8 minutes then add the chicken. Cook for 5 minutes then add the
spice blend, lentils, apricots and lemon juice. Stir in the stock or water and
simmer for 15 minutes.

Stir in the herbs and pomegranate seeds (if using) and serve with rice
or couscous.

Per serving 295 kcals, **protein** 41.6g, **carbohydrate** 28.3g, **fat** 2.5g, **saturated fat** 0.6g, **fibre** 3.6g, **salt** 0.29g

Chicken laksa

30 minutes | serves 4 | easy

4 skinless chicken thigh
   fillets, cut into cubes
2–3 tbsp laksa paste
400ml chicken stock
400ml coconut milk
2 kaffir lime leaves,
   finely shredded
200g beansprouts
200g cooked rice or
   egg noodles
1 red chilli, finely sliced,
   to serve
fish sauce, to season

A quick laksa recipe. Cook the chicken and laksa paste together with beansprouts, kaffir lime leaves and coconut milk for an easy and healthy Thai one pot for the family or as a casual dinner party dish for friends.

Put the chicken and paste in a pan and heat them gently, turning the chicken in the paste. Stir in the chicken stock and bring everything to a simmer. Add the coconut milk and lime leaves and simmer for 5 minutes, then add the beansprouts and cook for 1 minute more. Divide the noodles between 4 bowls and divide the laksa between them. Sprinkle with chilli to serve and season with fish sauce.

Per serving 527 kcals, **protein** 30.2g, **carbohydrate** 40g, **fat** 26.4g, **saturated fat** 17.1g, **fibre** 3.9g, **salt** 1g

Red pepper salad with baked chicken

1 hour | serves 4 | easy

3 red peppers, deseeded
   and cut into thick slices
1 red onion, finely sliced
olive oil
8 chicken pieces (whole
   legs and thighs)
2 tbsp ras el hanout
2 tbsp non-pareil capers
bunch of parsley, chopped
grated zest and juice of
   1 orange
salt and freshly ground
   black pepper

This red pepper citrus chicken is an easy one pan dish and requires little hands-on time.

Preheat the oven to 200°C/Fan 180°C/Gas 6. Tip the peppers into an ovenproof dish and scatter over the red onion. Add a good glug of olive oil, season well and stir everything together. Rub the chicken pieces with oil and sprinkle with a little ras el hanout, season, then sit them on top of the peppers and onion. Roast for 40–50 minutes or until the chicken is cooked through.

Lift the chicken off the peppers and transfer to serving plates. Add the capers, parsley and orange zest and juice to the peppers and serve with the chicken.

Per serving 521 kcals, **protein** 40.6g, **carbohydrate** 13.6g, **fat** 33.9g, **saturated fat** 8.8g, **fibre** 5g, **salt** 0.9g

Roast chicken and Jerusalem artichokes with lemon and sage butter

1 hour | serves 6 | easy

6 chicken breasts, skin on
butter, for cooking
400g Jerusalem artichokes
olive oil, for cooking
pared rind and juice of
  1 lemon
14 sage leaves
salt and freshly ground
  black pepper

This is a great alternative to your usual roast chicken. The flavours work brilliantly together.

Preheat the oven to 180°C/Fan 160°C/Gas 4. Rub each chicken breast with some butter and season them well. Peel the artichokes and quarter them. Toss them in some olive oil and season them well, then tip the artichokes into a roasting tin or baking dish so they fit in a snug single layer. Tuck the pieces of lemon rind and 8 of the sage leaves in among the artichokes. Roast for 20 minutes.

Put the chicken breasts on top and lay a sage leaf dipped in oil on top of each. Roast for 15 minutes and then turn the oven up to 200°C/Fan 180°C/Gas 6 for 10–15 minutes until the skin is golden, the chicken is cooked and the artichokes are tender. Squeeze over the lemon juice to serve.

Per serving 323 kcals, **protein** 37.4g, **carbohydrate** 7.5g, **fat** 15.2g, **saturated fat** 4.3g, **fibre** 3.1g, **salt** 0.3g

Barley risotto with chicken, broad beans and kale

1 hour | serves 6 | a little effort

2 tbsp butter

1 tbsp rapeseed oil

6 chicken thighs on
the bone

2 tbsp plain flour

½ tsp ground mace

2 onions, diced

2 garlic cloves, crushed

300g pearl barley

1.2 litres chicken stock

350g podded broad beans
(double-podded if
you like)

30g kale, tough stalks
removed and leaves
roughly chopped

grated zest and juice of
1 lemon

75g crème fraîche,
plus 6 tbsp to serve

few pinches of sweet
smoked paprika

salt and freshly ground
black pepper

Broad beans are in season from June to September, and this recipe for creamy but fresh barley risotto is a great way to make the most of them while they are at their best.

Heat half the butter and the oil in a casserole or deep frying pan. Toss the chicken thighs in the flour and ground mace to coat, then fry over a medium heat until golden brown and crisp on both sides. Lift onto a plate and tip the onions, garlic and the remaining tablespoon of butter into the pan and fry the vegetables until soft.

When the onion is really soft, return the chicken thighs to the pan with any juices, the barley and stock. Gently simmer for about 40 minutes, stirring occasionally, until the barley is almost tender and most of the stock has been absorbed. If it gets at all dry during cooking, add a splash more stock. Stir the broad beans, kale, lemon zest and juice and some seasoning into the barley, lower the heat and cover with a lid or baking sheet.

Meanwhile, skin the chicken thighs and shred the meat from the bones using a couple of forks. Stir the chicken back into the barley with the 75g of crème fraîche and check the beans and barley are both tender.

Spoon the barley into 6 shallow serving bowls. Top each serving with a spoon more of crème fraîche speckled with a pinch of paprika.

Per serving 617 kcals, **protein** 28.9g, **carbohydrate** 52.8g, **fat** 30.9g, **saturated fat** 14.7g, **fibre** 6.4g, **salt** 0.8g

Very quick chicken casserole

30 minutes | serves 2 | easy

4 large or 6 small skinless
  chicken thigh fillets
3 shallots, quartered
1 carrot, peeled and sliced
8 new potatoes or salad
  potatoes, skin left on,
  halved or quartered
  if large
500ml chicken stock
150g frozen peas
small bunch of tarragon,
  chopped
1 tbsp half-fat crème
  fraîche (optional)
salt and freshly ground
  black pepper

We know you love this classic *olive* recipe. A great one pot dish, our quick and easy chicken casserole makes a delicious midweek meal that is really hearty and comforting.

Put the chicken thighs, shallots, carrot, potatoes, some seasoning and the stock in a wide casserole and bring to a simmer. Cover and cook for 15 minutes, then add the peas and tarragon and cook for a further 10 minutes or until the potato is tender. Stir in the crème fraîche, if you like, then serve.

Per serving 412 kcals, **protein** 50.7g, **carbohydrate** 38.8g, **fat** 7.1g, **saturated fat** 2.4g, **fibre** 6.7g, **salt** 1.81g

Thai butternut and chicken red curry

30 minutes | serves 4 | easy

3–4 tbsp Thai red
  curry paste
oil, for frying (optional)
400ml can coconut milk
400g butternut squash,
  peeled and cubed
6 skinless chicken thighs,
  cut into cubes
250g cherry tomatoes
fish sauce, to season
2 limes, 1 juiced and
  1 quartered, to serve
2 large handfuls of Thai
  basil or coriander leaves

Whip up a delicious curry with butternut squash, chicken thighs, cherry tomatoes and coconut milk. This Thai recipe couldn't be simpler and is perfect served with coconut rice.

Heat the curry paste gently in a wok until it starts to fry in its own oil, adding a little extra oil if it starts to stick. Add the coconut milk and bring to a simmer. Add the squash and simmer for 10 minutes or until it is almost tender. Add the chicken and cook for 5 minutes, then add the cherry tomatoes and cook for 2 minutes or until they just start to burst.

Season with fish sauce (this is the equivalent of salt, so add a few drops and taste, then add more if you need it) and the lime juice and sprinkle with the herbs. Serve with the lime quarters for squeezing over.

Per serving 386 kcals, **protein** 32.1g, **carbohydrate** 13.9g, **fat** 22.8g, **saturated fat** 15.7g, **fibre** 2.2g, **salt** 1.26g

Chicken jalfrezi

45 minutes | serves 4 | easy

2 tbsp groundnut oil

1 large onion, halved and sliced

2–3 green chillies, sliced

3 garlic cloves, crushed

1 tbsp finely grated fresh root ginger

6 skinless chicken thigh fillets, cut into chunks

5 tomatoes, roughly chopped

1 green pepper, deseeded and chopped into pieces

small pot of natural yoghurt (optional)

small bunch of coriander, leaves picked

naan breads or steamed rice, to serve

salt and freshly ground black pepper

For the spice mix

1 tsp turmeric

1½ tsp ground cumin

1 tsp ground coriander

1 cinnamon stick

5 cloves, ground

Made with cheap chicken thigh fillets and a made-from-scratch spice blend, this easy, good-value curry is best served with basmati rice or naan.

Heat the oil in a large pan. Add the onion and a good pinch of salt, then fry for 6–8 minutes until golden.

Add the chillies, garlic and ginger. Cook for 3–4 minutes. Add the spice mix and cook for another couple of minutes until fragrant.

Add the chicken and cook for 3–4 minutes, then add the tomatoes, green pepper and a splash of water and stir well. Cover the pan and cook for about 30 minutes until the chicken is tender and the sauce thickened (uncover the pan if you need to for the last 10 minutes). Stir in the yoghurt (if using), off of the heat for a creamier sauce. Stir in the coriander and check the seasoning. Serve with naans or steamed rice.

Per serving 250 kcals, **protein** 29.2g, **carbohydrate** 10.5g, **fat** 10.4g, **saturated fat** 2.5g, **fibre** 2.5g, **salt** 0.34g

Poule au pot

2 hours 45 minutes | serves 6 | easy

1 celery stick, halved

3 sprigs of thyme

3 bay leaves

1 large chicken (about 2kg)

½ bottle white wine

50ml water

8 shallots, peeled and halved

3 cloves

4 small carrots, sliced

2 leeks, sliced

750g new potatoes, peeled and halved if large

200g self-raising flour

100g suet (pre-prepared suet is fine)

salt and freshly ground black pepper

For the stuffing

200g pork mince or sausage meat

100g thick-cut bacon, diced

3–4 chicken livers, chopped (optional)

few sage leaves, chopped

1 egg, beaten

2 garlic cloves, finely chopped

6 shallots, diced

bunch of flat-leaf parsley, chopped

2 big handfuls of fresh breadcrumbs

This is a great one pot dish for feeding a crowd. Serve with some of the cooking liquid – the rest makes a delicious broth or stock.

Tie the celery together with the thyme and the bay leaves to make a bouquet garni. Preheat the oven to 190°C/Fan 170°C/Gas 5. To make the stuffing, put all the ingredients into a bowl and mix together really well.

Trim the chicken cavity of any excess fat and fill with the stuffing. Close up and secure with a couple of skewers. Put the chicken in a large casserole with a lid. Add the wine, water, shallots, bouquet garni, cloves and some seasoning. Cover with the lid and cook in the oven for 1 hour.

Add the carrots, leeks and potatoes to the pot, put the lid back on and return to the oven for 1 hour.

Combine the flour and suet with some seasoning. Add enough cold water to make a firm but pliable dough. Divide into 12 dumplings.

Remove the casserole from the oven. Carefully transfer the chicken to a plate, cover with foil and keep warm. Add the dumplings to the pot, replace the lid and put back in the oven for 20–25 minutes until the dumplings are cooked.

To serve, take the skin off the chicken and remove the meat from the bones. Divide the chicken, stuffing, veg and dumplings between warmed bowls. Spoon over some of the cooking juices and serve.

Per serving 971 kcals, **protein** 61g, **carbohydrate** 62.5g, **fat** 52.6g, **saturated fat** 18.1g, **fibre** 4.4g, **salt** 1.6g

Rosemary salt roast chicken

1 hour 20 minutes, plus overnight salting | serves 4 | easy

1 whole chicken
   (about 1.5kg)
1 tbsp flaked sea salt
1 tbsp chopped rosemary
   leaves, plus 2 whole
   sprigs
olive oil, for brushing

Rubbing the chicken with salt and rosemary and leaving it overnight really makes a world of difference: the salt tenderises the bird and the flavour of rosemary permeates the meat.

The day before you want to cook the chicken, rub it all over with the sea salt and chopped rosemary. Put it in a large plastic freezer bag, seal and leave overnight (or sit it in a dish and cover with cling film).

The next day, brush off any salty, herby residue with kitchen paper and leave the chicken to sit at room temperature for 1 hour.

Preheat the oven to 200°C/Fan 180°C/Gas 6. Brush the chicken lightly with olive oil. Put the chicken in a roasting tin, put the rosemary sprigs in and around the bird and cook for 1 hour 15 minutes, or until the chicken has a crisp, golden skin and is cooked through. To check if it is done, pierce the fattest part of the thigh with a skewer – the juices should run clear. If they don't, give it another 10 minutes in the oven. Rest the chicken for 20 minutes, covered loosely with foil, before carving.

Per serving 385 kcals, **protein** 40.5g, **carbohydrate** 0.3g, **fat** 24.6g, **saturated fat** 8g, **fibre** 0g, **salt** 2.9g

Sunday chicken

2 hours 10 minutes | serves 4 | easy

1 onion, peeled and halved
1 garlic head, halved
   crosswise
2 sprigs of thyme
1 sprig of rosemary
1 sprig of sage
1 large whole chicken
olive oil
1 litre chicken stock
salt and freshly ground
   black pepper

For the stuffing

50g butter
1 onion, finely diced
1 garlic clove, finely diced
2 sprigs of sage, chopped
a handful of mixed
   mushrooms (wild,
   if possible), roughly
   chopped
120g sourdough bread,
   crusts removed, cut into
   1cm dice
handful of ready-cooked
   and peeled chestnuts,
   crushed
1 egg
3 Cumberland sausages,
   skin removed

This is a clever makeover of the classic roast chicken. The mushrooms and chestnuts really bump up the flavour in the stuffing.

First, make the stuffing. Melt the butter in a frying pan, and cook the onion and garlic until soft and translucent. Season. Add the sage and the mushrooms, and continue to cook until soft. Add the bread and allow to soak up any butter, then transfer to a mixing bowl. Add the chestnuts, and give it all a good mix. Cool, then add the egg and sausage meat and mix well. Chill.

Heat the oven to 180°C/Fan 160°C/Gas 4. Make sure any giblets are removed from the chicken, and fill the cavity with the stuffing.

Put the onion, garlic and herbs into a roasting tin. Put the chicken on top and drizzle with olive oil. Season well and put in the oven. After about 40 minutes, the chicken will be nice and brown: at this point add half the stock, then lower the oven temperature to 160°C/Fan 140°C/Gas 3 and roast for a further 50 minutes or until cooked. (Check by piercing the thickest part of the thigh – if the juices do not run clear, put it back in the oven for 10 minutes.)

Take the chicken out of the roasting tin to rest, add the remaining stock to the tin (or tip it into a pan) and turn the heat up to high. Reduce rapidly until you have a gravy consistency. Strain, and serve alongside the carved chicken.

Per serving 756 kcals, **protein** 59.8g, **carbohydrate** 30.7g, **fat** 42.7g, **saturated fat** 16.5g, **fibre** 5.1g, **salt** 2.5g

Turkey chilli bean stew

35 minutes | serves 2 | easy

1 tbsp olive oil

1 large onion, chopped

2 garlic cloves, crushed

1 carrot, peeled and cut
into small dice

1 celery stick, cut into
small dice

2 tbsp chipotle paste or
2 tsp hot smoked paprika

1 green pepper, deseeded
and cut into chunks

400g can chopped
tomatoes

400ml chicken stock

400g can black beans,
drained and rinsed

200g cooked turkey or
chicken, torn into chunks

small bunch of coriander,
chopped, to serve

crusty bread, to serve

salt and freshly ground
black pepper

**This is a good way of using up cooked meat over the holidays –
at other times of the year, chicken or ham work nicely as well.
The chipotle paste and smoked paprika gives this a lovely smoky,
but not too hot, chilli flavour.**

Heat the olive oil in a pan. Cook the onion, garlic, carrot and celery for
5 minutes until softened. Add the chipotle paste or paprika and green
pepper and cook for 1 minute. Stir in the tomatoes and stock and bring to
a simmer. Add the beans and cook for 20 minutes until the sauce thickens.
Stir in the turkey and simmer for 5 minutes.

Sprinkle with coriander, season and serve in bowls with crusty bread.

Per serving 503 kcals, **protein** 50.1g, **carbohydrate** 39.6g, **fat** 11.8g, **saturated fat** 2.6g, **fibre** 1.9g, **salt** 2g

Roast cardamom and chilli butter-basted guinea fowl

1½ hours | serves 3-4 | easy

1 guinea fowl

3 tbsp mascarpone

50g butter

6 cardamom pods,
   lightly crushed

large pinch of dried
   red chilli flakes

2 shallots, peeled and
   quartered

salt and freshly ground
   black pepper

Guinea fowl is as easy to cook as chicken and will make a stunning and unusual dinner party main course. Here the bird is flavoured with a cardamom and chilli butter.

Preheat the oven to 200°C/Fan 180°C/Gas 6. Wipe the guinea fowl dry, untie and season the skin well. Put the mascarpone into the cavity of the body and sit the bird in a shallow casserole. Heat the butter in a small pan with the cardamom and chilli until the butter melts, then brush it all over the guinea fowl, keeping some aside, and put the bird into the oven for 20 minutes. Baste again and cook for a further 20 minutes.

Turn the oven down to 180°C/Fan 160°C/Gas 4 and baste the bird again with the remaining butter, tipping the spices out onto the skin. Tip the shallots into the juices that have formed in the base of the pan and cook for a further 20 minutes.

Rest the bird for 20 minutes, then tip any juices from the guinea fowl back into the pan before lifting it out. Heat the juice until it bubbles. Carve the guinea fowl and add any carving juices to the sauce, then spoon these over to serve.

Per serving (3) 405 kcals, **protein** 37.7g, **carbohydrate** 1.4g, **fat** 27.5g, **saturated fat** 16.4g, **fibre** 0.2g, **salt** 0.6g

Braised rabbit with prunes and white wine

2 hours | serves 4 | easy

4 rabbit legs

oil, for frying

8 shallots, peeled

8 small carrots, peeled

2 bay leaves

large sprig of thyme

8 ready-to-eat prunes

250ml white wine

250–400ml chicken stock

mash or pasta, to serve

salt and freshly ground
   black pepper

This recipe for braised rabbit with prunes and white wine is a really easy one pot that delivers fantastic big flavours. Serve simply with mash or pasta for a fuss-free family meal.

Season the rabbit legs well all over. Heat a little oil in a casserole or large heavy pan with a lid and fry the rabbit legs until they are lightly browned all over. Add the shallots and carrots and fry briefly, then add the bay leaves, thyme, prunes and white wine and bubble everything together for 1 minute. Add enough chicken stock to cover the rabbit legs and bring the contents of the pan to a simmer. Cover and cook for 1½ hours.

Take off the lid and turn the heat up a little to slightly reduce the liquid. Taste it – when the sauce has a good strong flavour it is ready. Serve with mash or pasta.

Per serving 301 kcals, **protein** 29.5g, **carbohydrate** 29.5g, **fat** 7.1g, **saturated fat** 2.6g, **fibre** 5.8g, **salt** 0.4g

Gamekeeper's pie

2½ hours | serves 6 | easy

750g ready prepared
　game, cut into large
　cubes (ask your butcher
　or look for packs in
　supermarkets)
2 tbsp plain flour
1 onion, finely sliced
1 carrot, peeled and sliced
500ml red wine
250ml strong beef stock
1 tbsp redcurrant jelly
1 bay leaf
1 large celeriac
1 large potato,
　peeled and cubed
1 garlic clove, peeled
knob of salted butter
salt and freshly ground
　black pepper

This is a great, easy way to enjoy beautiful fresh game in the winter months.

Preheat the oven to 160°C/Fan 140°C/Gas 3. Toss the game pieces with the flour and plenty of seasoning and tip them into a casserole with onion and carrot, then add the red wine, stock and redcurrant jelly along with the bay leaf and stir well. Bring to a simmer on the stovetop. Cover and cook in the oven for 1 hour, then take off the lid and cook for another hour, or until tender and the liquid has reduced to make a thick gravy.

Meanwhile, peel and cube the celeriac and cook it in simmering water with the potato and garlic until it is tender. This will take about 40 minutes. Drain well and mash thoroughly, adding plenty of seasoning and a very large knob of butter.

Turn the oven up to 200°C/Fan 180°C/Gas 6. Spoon the mash over the game mixture, dot with more butter and cook for 10 minutes, or until the top starts to brown.

Per serving 352 kcals, **protein** 31.6g, **carbohydrate** 17.4g, **fat** 10.2g, **saturated fat** 4.5g, **fibre** 5.7g, **salt** 0.7g

Pork, lamb and beef

Pea and coriander soup with chorizo

30 minutes | serves 4 | easy

1 tbsp olive oil

60g pack sliced chorizo,
  cut into strips

1 onion, roughly chopped

knob of butter, for frying

1 medium potato,
  peeled and diced

750ml chicken stock

400g frozen peas

½ small bunch of coriander,
  roughly chopped

A bag of frozen peas can be turned into a vibrant green bowl of goodness with this delicious and easy soup. Chorizo is the secret ingredient and lends an interesting saltiness to the veg. You don't need to use much so it keeps the calories down, too. Serve with crusty bread on the side.

Heat the oil in a pan and cook the chorizo until crisp. Set aside.

In the same pan, cook the onion with the butter until softened. Add the potato and cook for a moment, then tip in the stock. Simmer until the potato is soft. Keep back a good handful of peas then add the rest to the pan and bring back to a simmer for 2 minutes. Add the coriander, stir until just wilted, then turn off the heat. Blend until smooth.

Stir the reserved peas into the soup, heat through and serve topped with the chorizo slices.

Per serving 214 kcals, **protein** 15.4g, **carbohydrate** 19.5g, **fat** 8.5g, **saturated fat** 2.9g, **fibre** 7.1g, **salt** 0.8g

Vermicelli meatball soup

30 minutes | serves 2 | easy

250g lean pork mince
1 garlic clove, crushed
½ small onion, grated
½ small bunch of parsley,
  chopped
pinch of dried chilli flakes
handful of fresh
  breadcrumbs
50g Parmesan,
  finely grated
1 tbsp olive oil
500ml chicken stock
50g vermicelli pasta,
  broken into pieces
salt and freshly ground
  black pepper

This soup is easy and filling. Serve with a generous sprinkling of Parmesan.

Put the pork mince, garlic, onion, half the parsley, the chilli flakes, breadcrumbs and half the Parmesan in a bowl. Mix using clean hands, season really well and form into little meatballs.

Heat the oil in a non-stick pan. Fry the meatballs until golden all over, then scoop out. Add the chicken stock to the pan and bring to a simmer. Add the vermicelli and cook for 1 minute. Return the meatballs to the pan and keep on a gentle simmer until the vermicelli is cooked through. Stir in the remaining parsley and serve in bowls with the rest of the Parmesan sprinkled over.

Per serving 482 kcals, **protein** 43.5g, **carbohydrate** 32.2g, **fat** 20.9g, **saturated fat** 7.8g, **fibre** 0.8g, **salt** 2.84g

Baked eggs with ratatouille and chorizo

30 minutes | serves 2 | easy

olive oil, for frying
150g chorizo, cut into
   small chunks
1 small aubergine,
   cut into chunks
1 courgette, cut into
   chunks
1 onion, finely chopped
2 garlic cloves, crushed
1 roasted red pepper
   from a jar, sliced
400g can chopped
   tomatoes
2 tsp sugar
1 tbsp sherry vinegar
handful of flat-leaf parsley,
   roughly chopped
2 eggs
salt and freshly ground
   black pepper

The best baked eggs recipe. Chorizo adds spice to a quick ratatouille made on the hob, then you pop it in the oven to cook the eggs. Ideal served with crusty bread.

Preheat the oven to 180°C/Fan 160°C/Gas 4. Heat 1 tablespoon of oil in an ovenproof frying pan or shallow casserole, add the chorizo and fry on all sides until crisp and the pan is collecting chorizo oil. Lift the slices from the pan, add the aubergine chunks and fry until golden, crisp on the outside and softening, then lift these from the pan, too. Repeat with the courgette.

Add 1 tablespoon of oil to the pan along with the onion and garlic and soften together. Return the aubergines with the courgettes, sliced pepper, tomatoes, sugar, vinegar, most of the chopped parsley and some seasoning. Simmer for 5 minutes, adding a splash of water if it's looking dry.

Make a couple of hollows in the ratatouille mixture and crack in the eggs, then scatter over the rest of the chorizo. Bake in the oven for 10–12 minutes or until the whites have just set. Scatter with the remaining parsley and some seasoning and serve with crusty bread for mopping up the juices.

Per serving 494 kcals, **protein** 26.6g, **carbohydrate** 25g, **fat** 29.9g, **saturated fat** 9.8g, **fibre** 9.2g, **salt** 1.5g

Storecupboard fried rice

20 minutes | serves 2 | easy

100g frozen peas

1 tbsp oil

4 spring onions,
   finely chopped

1 garlic clove, crushed

small chunk of fresh root
   ginger, peeled and grated

2–3 slices ham or bacon,
   cut into pieces

250g cooked rice
   (use leftovers or a bag
   of microwaveable rice)

1 egg, beaten with 2 tsp
   sesame oil

chilli sauce and soy sauce,
   to serve

This is a really useful recipe on those days when you're too busy to shop for specific ingredients. You're likely to have everything you need for this dish already, and it's on the table in under 30 minutes. The perfect hassle-free meal.

Put the peas in a colander and pour over a kettle of boiling water to defrost.

Heat the oil in a wok or large frying pan. Cook the spring onions for 2 minutes then add the garlic and ginger and cook for 1 minute. Stir in the ham or bacon and peas and fry for a couple of minutes (longer if you are using bacon). Add the rice and cook until heated through, then tip in the egg and stir through until just set. Spoon into bowls and serve the chilli and soy sauce on the side for seasoning.

Per serving 367 kcals, **protein** 18g, **carbohydrate** 40.4g, **fat** 14.1g, **saturated fat** 2.7g, **fibre** 4.4g, **salt** 1.1g

Slow-cooked pork carnitas with tomatillo salsa

5 hours | serves 10 | easy

2kg skinless pork shoulder,
  cut into 10cm pieces
1 tbsp ground cumin
1½ tbsp ground coriander
1 cinnamon stick
2 bay leaves
1 onion, quartered
4 garlic cloves, left whole
juice of 2 large oranges
salt and freshly ground
  black pepper

For the salsa

1 large or 2 smaller tins
  tomatillos, drained,
  or 6–8 large green/unripe
  tomatoes
3 garlic cloves, skin on
3 green chillies, halved
  lengthways
1 onion, peeled and
  quartered
handful of coriander leaves
olive oil

To serve

warm tortillas, finely sliced
  red onion, crumbled feta,
  lime wedges, coriander
  leaves

Carnitas are the next step up from tacos. Traditionally cooked slowly in fat, the meat is meltingly tender. This is a lighter version. You can buy tomatillos online or replace them with chopped tomatoes. It needs a little prep but then can all be cooked in one pot.

Preheat the oven to 220°C/Fan 200°C/Gas 7. To make the salsa, put the tomatillos, garlic, chillies and onion on a baking sheet. Season and toss with a little olive oil then roast in the oven for 15–20 minutes, until the onion, garlic and chillies are really soft and a little charred at the edges. Peel the roasted garlic and discard the chilli stems, then tip everything into a food processor with the coriander and whizz until blended.

Lower the oven temperature to 130°C/Fan 110°C/Gas 1. Toss the pork with some seasoning and the cumin and coriander. Put in the bottom of a very large shallow casserole or baking dish and tuck in the cinnamon, bay leaves, onion and garlic. Pour over the orange juice. Put on a lid or tightly cover with foil then cook in the oven for 4 hours.

Take off the lid and turn up the oven to 200°C/Fan 180°C/Gas 6. Pour off the excess liquid from the meat into a jug and discard the cinnamon stick. Cook for another 20–30 minutes until the pork starts to crisp up at the edges. Roughly shred the pork, adding a few spoons of the reserved liquid, then pile into warm tortillas with the salsa and accompaniments.

Per serving 312 kcals, **protein** 28.3g, **carbohydrate** 7.2g, **fat** 18.5g, **saturated fat** 5.8g, **fibre** 1.7g, **salt** 0.2g

Sticky pork and mangetout stir-fry

20 minutes | serves 2 | easy

100g dried egg noodles
300g pork escalopes,
   cut into strips
1 tsp cornflour
1 tbsp oil
4 spring onions, shredded
100g mangetout,
   halved lengthways
juice of 1 lemon
1 tbsp honey
2 tbsp soy sauce
2 tbsp sweet chilli sauce
salt and freshly ground
   black pepper

Pork, noodles, mangetout: the three main ingredients for this quick and easy stir-fry. Spice it up with sweet chilli sauce to serve and tuck in for a fast and satisfying meal for two.

Cook the noodles and drain well. Toss the pork with the cornflour and some seasoning.

Heat the oil in a wok or large non-stick frying pan and stir-fry the pork for 2 minutes then scoop out the meat. Add the veg to the pan, keeping back some of the spring onions, and toss for a couple of minutes.

Add back the pork and the lemon juice, honey, soy and chilli sauces, plus a splash of water, and bubble for a few minutes until you have a sauce. Toss with the noodles until heated through and sprinkle over the reserved spring onions to serve.

Per serving 594 kcals, **protein** 37.6g, **carbohydrate** 49.4g, **fat** 26.5g, **saturated fat** 7.3g, **fibre** 3.8g, **salt** 3.9g

Gammon with leeks

30 minutes | serves 2 | easy

1 potato, very thinly sliced
1 leek, cleaned, trimmed
   and thinly sliced
300ml fresh chicken stock,
   or made with a cube or
   concentrate
1 tsp coriander seeds
2 gammon steaks or slices
Dijon mustard, to serve
freshly ground black
   pepper

Gammon and leeks make a classic combination. This easy one pot marries fantastic flavours and is a comforting, speedy supper for an autumnal night.

Put the potato, leek, chicken stock and coriander seeds in a wok or frying pan. Season with black pepper. Boil for 5–6 minutes until the vegetables are just tender. Put the gammon on top of the vegetables and cook for 6 minutes.

Finish under the grill until it just begins to crisp. Either stir the mustard into the stock sauce or serve it on the side.

Per serving 344 kcals, **protein** 39.4g, **carbohydrate** 18.8g, **fat** 12.9g, **saturated fat** 3.6g, **fibre** 1.6g, **salt** 3.76g

Radicchio and pancetta risotto

40 minutes | serves 2 | easy

4-6 slices smoked
   pancetta, thinly sliced
25g butter, plus a small
   knob
2 tbsp olive oil
4 shallots, finely diced
75g smoked pancetta,
   diced
1 radicchio (about 225g)
225g risotto rice
500-600ml hot chicken
   stock
2 tbsp full-fat crème
   fraîche
25-50g Parmesan,
   finely grated
salt and freshly ground
   black pepper

Radicchio and pancetta are a classic Italian pairing. Sharp and salty, they have been brought together to complement this creamy risotto.

Heat a small casserole and dry-fry the pancetta slices until the fat turns golden. Remove from the dish and set aside – they will go crisp. Melt the butter and heat the oil in the casserole. Add the shallots and fry gently until soft. Add the diced pancetta and continue to cook, stirring, until almost crisp.

In the meantime, cut the top half off the radicchio and shred. Slice the bottom half into thin wedges, trimming the root but leaving enough of it behind to hold the wedges together.

Add the rice to the pan, stir briskly for a minute or two, then add the shredded radicchio and a ladleful of stock. Cook at a gentle simmer, stirring from time to time, adding more stock as each addition is absorbed.

If you like your radicchio charred, heat a cast-iron griddle pan and cook the radicchio wedges on both sides so they are slightly charred. Remove and set aside.

When the rice is nearly cooked but still has a good bite, about 20 minutes, check for seasoning, turn off the heat, add the crème fraîche and the extra butter, stir well, put the lid on the casserole and leave for 5 minutes.

Just before serving, stir in the radicchio wedges. Top each plateful with the crisp pancetta and Parmesan.

Per serving 1,196 kcals, **protein** 41.1g, **carbohydrate** 91.7g, **fat** 72.9g, **saturated fat** 32.6g, **fibre** 4.3g, **salt** 4.7g

Spelt risotto with pancetta and peas

30 minutes | serves 2 | easy

butter, for frying and
    finishing
1 onion, finely chopped
70g cubetti di pancetta
1 garlic clove, sliced
150g pearled spelt
glass of white wine
500–750ml hot chicken
    stock
handful of frozen peas
50g Grana Padano,
    finely grated
salt and freshly ground
    black pepper

Call this a speltotto or spelt risotto, it doesn't matter, either will deliver a bowl of comforting carbohydrate to warm you up on a cold night. Spelt has a more nutty flavour than rice. Look for pearled spelt, which has had the outer husk removed so it cooks more quickly.

Melt a knob of butter in a shallow, wide pan. Add the onion and cook until softened. Add the pancetta and cook for 3–4 minutes until it starts to crisp up. Add the garlic and cook for 2 minutes. Tip in the spelt and stir.

Turn up the heat then tip in the wine, stirring until it has been absorbed, then add the stock bit by bit, as with risotto rice, until it is all absorbed and the spelt is tender, about 20 minutes (you might need a bit more stock or water). Add the peas when the spelt is nearly tender, with the last bit of stock.

To finish, stir in another knob of butter and the cheese, then taste and season, if needed.

Per serving 634 kcals, **protein** 28.1g, **carbohydrate** 59.1g, **fat** 29.7g, **saturated fat** 15.1g, **fibre** 6.6g, **salt** 4.42g

Pasta with crisp chorizo, olive oil and parsley

20 minutes | serves 2 | easy

3 tbsp olive oil

1 pack sliced chorizo (around 70g), cut into strips

1 red chilli, finely chopped

1 garlic clove, crushed

150g cooked spaghetti

2 tbsp water

½ small bunch of flat-leaf parsley, chopped

salt and freshly ground black pepper

Chorizo adds enough saltiness to act as a base for this pasta. Cook your pasta first then toss it with the chorizo and olive oil to save adding extra oil and for ease of washing up!

Heat the oil in a pan and cook the chorizo until crisp. Add the chilli and garlic and cook for a minute.

Tip the pasta and water into the chorizo pan with the parsley and some seasoning. Toss together, then serve.

Per serving 461 kcals, **protein** 15.2g, **carbohydrate** 41.4g, **fat** 26.5g, **saturated fat** 5.7g, **fibre** 0.6g, **salt** 0.6g

Smoked ham hock and barley risotto primavera

3 hours, plus cooling | serves 6 | easy

1 smoked ham hock,
   soaked overnight
   if needed
1 carrot
3 medium onions,
   1 halved, 2 finely diced
100g unsalted butter
2 garlic cloves
sprig of thyme,
   leaves finely chopped
200g risotto rice
200g pearl barley
150g frozen peas
150g broad beans,
   double-podded if
   you like
6 asparagus spears,
   sliced on an angle
20 green beans, cut into
   short lengths
4 spring onions, sliced on
   an angle
100g mascarpone
85g Parmesan, grated
salt and freshly ground
   black pepper

A mix of risotto rice and pearl barley makes a lovely nutty risotto. Ask your butcher if you need to soak the smoked ham hock overnight to remove any excess saltiness, as this will affect the finished stock.

Put the ham hock into a pot full of clean, cold water with the carrot and halved onion. Bring to a simmer and cook for 2½ hours, skimming the surface now and again. Top up the pan with water if needed. Remove the ham from the pan and strain the stock.

Melt the butter in a heavy-based pan and add the diced onions, garlic and thyme. Cook until softened but not coloured. Add the rice and the pearl barley and cook for a couple of minutes until coated in the butter. Gradually add the stock from the ham and vegetables, stirring throughout. After about 10 minutes, add the green veg, apart from the spring onions. Cook for another 5–10 minutes, still stirring and simmering until you have used nearly all of the stock and the veg are tender.

Taste your risotto and if you are happy with the texture, reduce to a medium heat and stir in the spring onions and ham and let everything heat through, then season.

Stir in the mascarpone and the grated Parmesan and serve.

Per serving 832 kcals, **protein** 33.9g, **carbohydrate** 63.8g, **fat** 49.9g, **saturated fat** 28.7g, **fibre** 6.5g, **salt** 2.6g

Pork with turnips

45 minutes | serves 4 | easy

6 small turnips, trimmed
   and halved
1 onion, chopped
olive oil
4 pork chops, fat trimmed
handful of sage leaves
2 oranges, grated zest of
   1 and juice of both
salt and freshly ground
   black pepper

The humble turnip gets a starring role in this easy one pot, pork chop roast with zingy orange and sage flavours. Halved small, sweet turnips work best for this but if you have larger ones, slice them thickly instead. Serve some simple buttered greens on the side for a family meal without the fuss.

Preheat the oven to 200°C/Fan 180°C/Gas 6. Boil the turnips for 5 minutes then drain. Fry the onion in a little olive oil in a pan and tip into a baking dish. Add the turnips and season. Fry the chops briefly in the same pan over a high heat just to colour them and put on top of the onions and turnips, season well.

Tuck the sage leaves around the chops and pour over the orange juice and zest. Drizzle over a little more oil and bake for 20-30 minutes, or until the chops are cooked throughout and browned.

Per serving 229 kcals, **protein** 25.7g, **carbohydrate** 12.3g, **fat** 8.9g, **saturated fat** 2g, **fibre** 4.1g, **salt** 0.24g

Sausages with sage and butternut

50 minutes | serves 4 | easy

8 pork sausages, skinned
small bunch of sage leaves,
  2 tbsp chopped
pinch of chilli flakes
olive oil, for frying
1 large onion, roughly
  chopped
1 butternut squash, peeled
  and cut into 2cm chunks
750ml chicken stock
salt and freshly ground
  black pepper

Teamed with butternut squash and sage, this is a new idea for sausages. This easy one pot freezes really well – just defrost overnight in the fridge then heat until piping hot. Serve with mash, rice or pasta on the side, or just as it is, with crusty bread to mop up the juices.

Put the sausage meat in a bowl and add the chopped sage, chilli flakes and some seasoning. Roll into walnut-sized balls then brown all over in a pan with a little olive oil. Scoop out, add the onion and cook until softened. Add the squash and cook until it just starts to turn golden, then add the sausage balls back and the stock. Simmer until the squash is tender.

Fry a few more whole sage leaves until crisp then top the stew with them.

Per serving 465 kcals, **protein** 22.1g, **carbohydrate** 33.5g, **fat** 27.3g, **saturated fat** 10.1g, **fibre** 8.4g, **salt** 3g

Smoky baked pork and beans

3½ hours | serves 6 | easy

2 tbsp olive oil

500g boneless rindless
   pork belly slices,
   cut into chunks

1 large onion, sliced

3 garlic cloves, crushed

1 tbsp English mustard
   powder

1 tbsp soft light brown
   sugar

1 tbsp black treacle
   or molasses

1 tsp hot smoked paprika

2 tsp ground cumin

2 tbsp tomato purée

2 tbsp tamarind paste

400g can chopped
   tomatoes

400g can pinto beans,
   drained and rinsed

600ml vegetable stock

2 bay leaves

2 sprigs of thyme

buttered crusty bread,
   to serve

Adding big chunks of pork belly to this classic American side dish upgrades it to a meal-in-a-bowl.

Preheat the oven to 140°C/Fan 120°C/Gas 2. Heat the oil in a large casserole. Add the pork and cook until crisp and golden. Add the onion and cook until soft, then add the garlic and cook for a further minute.

Add the mustard, sugar, treacle or molasses, smoked paprika, cumin, tomato purée, tamarind paste and chopped tomatoes to the pan, stir well and cook for 30 seconds. Add the beans and stock, the bay leaves and thyme. Mix well, bring to the boil and cover with a tight-fitting lid. Cook in the oven for 3 hours until the beans are tender and the sauce thickened.

Serve in bowls with a spoon and some buttered crusty bread.

Per serving 468 kcals, **protein** 29.1g, **carbohydrate** 48.9g, **fat** 17g, **saturated fat** 4.6g, **fibre** 1.7g, **salt** 0.3g

Pinto bean and spicy sausage chilli

1 hour | serves 4 | easy

6 spicy pork sausages

1 onion, finely chopped

2 garlic cloves, crushed

1 green pepper, deseeded
   and cut into chunks

2 tsp ground cumin

big pinch of chilli flakes

2 x 400g cans chopped
   tomatoes

1 tsp caster sugar

400g can pinto beans,
   drained and rinsed

handful of coriander,
   chopped, plus extra
   leaves to garnish

150g cooked basmati rice,
   to serve

soured cream, to serve

salt and freshly ground
   black pepper

You'll need some nice spicy sausages for this – you can try fresh pork chorizo-style sausages, but anything with a decent chilli and herb content will do.

Cook the sausages in a wide pan with a lid until browned all over and cooked through. Take out of the pan and add the onion, garlic and pepper. Cook for 5 minutes until softened then add the cumin and chillies. Cook for a minute then add the tomatoes and sugar. Stir, season and bring to a simmer.

Slice the sausages into chunks on an angle then add back to the sauce with the beans. Simmer for 30 minutes until the sauce has thickened. Stir in the chopped coriander. Serve with rice, soured cream and scatter with coriander leaves.

Per serving 385 kcals, **protein** 22.5g, **carbohydrate** 31g, **fat** 19.9g, **saturated fat** 6g, **fibre** 8.5g, **salt** 1.54g

Slow-roast pork with chilli and orange

6 hours, plus marinating | serves 8 | easy

1 boneless rolled pork
  shoulder (about 2kg)
grated zest and juice of
  2 oranges
2 tbsp soft light brown
  sugar
1 tbsp light miso paste
2 dried red chillies
1 onion, sliced
1 red chilli, diced
baked potatoes or buns,
  to serve

Slow-roasting pork shoulder at a low temperature turns a tough, economical cut into tender 'pulled pork'. Try something a bit different here with the flavours of miso, chilli and orange.

Dry the pork shoulder skin with kitchen paper, score it with a very sharp knife and put it in a roasting tin. Mix the orange zest and juice with the sugar and miso and add the dried red chillies. Pour this over the pork, cover and leave overnight at room temperature, or for several hours.

Preheat the oven to 150°C/Fan 130°C/Gas 2. Lift the pork and lay the onion slices in the roasting tin and put the pork on top, skin side up. Add a mug of water to the marinade in the tin. Cover the lot with foil and cook for 4 hours.

Take off the foil and turn the oven up to 180°C/Fan 160°C/Gas 4. Baste the pork with any juices and cook it for a further hour, then turn the oven up again to 200°C/Fan 180°C/Gas 6. Add more water if you need to, to make sure the juices don't burn. Cook for 30 minutes to make sure the skin crisps. Lift the pork onto a plate to rest, pour the juices into the bowl and add the fresh chilli.

Pull the pork into chunks and dress them with the juices and add the cooked onion, if you like. Serve stuffed into baked potatoes or bread buns.

Per serving 456 kcals, **protein** 45.2g, **carbohydrate** 7.8g, **fat** 27g, **saturated fat** 9.3g, **fibre** 0.5g, **salt** 0.5g

Chickpea and merguez stew with chilli garlic oil

2½ hours, plus soaking time | serves 6 | easy

12 merguez sausages

olive oil, for frying

2 onions, finely chopped

6 garlic cloves,
    very thinly sliced

3 celery sticks,
    finely chopped

5 carrots, peeled and
    finely diced

few sprigs of thyme

1 tbsp tomato purée

200ml white wine

300g dried chickpeas,
    soaked in cold water
    in the fridge overnight

500ml chicken stock

125ml extra virgin olive oil

1 tbsp dried chilli flakes

handful of flat-leaf parsley,
    roughly chopped

salt and freshly ground
    black pepper

Good butchers and larger supermarkets will sell spicy lamb merguez sausages, or you could substitute them with cooking chorizo sausages if you like.

Brown the sausages all over in a little oil in a large casserole or saucepan, remove, slice into chunks and set aside.

Put 2 tablespoons of olive oil into the casserole or saucepan and tip in the onions, half the garlic, celery and carrots. Cook the veg for 15 minutes or until tender. Add the thyme and tomato purée. Cook for 1 minute more.

Pour over the wine and let it bubble down for a few minutes. Drain and rinse the soaked chickpeas then add them to the pan with the chicken stock. Top up with 1 litre of cold water so the chickpeas are covered, and bring to a boil. Skim off any scum that comes to the surface. Turn down the heat and simmer for 1½–2 hours or until the chickpeas are soft, adding a little more water if they look like they are drying out.

Add the browned sausages to the chickpeas. Cover the pot and cook for 20 minutes more, until the sausages are cooked through. Take off the lid and simmer until the liquid has thickened and reduced.

Meanwhile, add the extra virgin olive oil to a saucepan. Scatter in the chilli flakes and remaining garlic. Warm over a low heat for about 10 minutes or until the garlic is completely softened, taking care not to let it burn. Season and stir through the parsley.

Spoon the stew into bowls and drizzle over the spicy oil.

Per serving 760 kcals, **protein** 31.2g, **carbohydrate** 45.5g, **fat** 48.5g, **saturated fat** 13.2g, **fibre** 9.5g, **salt** 2.6g

Sausage, beetroot and red cabbage hotpot

2 hours | serves 4 | easy

½ red cabbage, core
  removed and leaves
  shredded
1 onion, grated
250g raw beetroot, peeled,
  half coarsely grated,
  half cut into 2cm chunks
125ml red wine vinegar
75g soft light brown sugar
100ml good-quality
  blackcurrant cordial
½ tsp ground allspice
250ml water
2 tsp olive oil
8 good-quality sausages
  (pork or venison)
100g raisins
mash or buttered soda
  bread, to serve
salt and freshly ground
  black pepper

The contrasting sweet and earthy flavours of this dish with the sausages will be a hit with the whole family. Plus it's really simple to make and requires minimal 'hands-on' time.

Tip the shredded cabbage into a large pan with a lid and stir in the onion, beetroot (grated and chunks), vinegar, sugar, cordial and allspice with the water and some seasoning. Bring to a simmer, then reduce the heat and cover with a lid. Cook gently for 1 hour 15 minutes.

After 1 hour, heat the oil in another pan and brown the sausages all over. Stir them into the cabbage with the raisins (plus a drop more water if it's looking dry), re-cover and cook for another 20–30 minutes, until the sausages are cooked through. Spoon into bowls with some mash, or eat with buttered soda bread.

Per serving 444 kcals, **protein** 24g, **carbohydrate** 68.5g, **fat** 6.9g, **saturated fat** 3g, **fibre** 6.3g, **salt** 1.4g

Lamb kofta in sweet-sour tomato sauce

50 minutes | serves 4 | easy

1 onion, finely chopped
oil, for frying
2 tsp ground cinnamon
1 tbsp ground cumin
500g lamb mince
3 tbsp pine nuts
400g can chopped
   tomatoes, roughly
   mashed
2 tsp golden caster sugar
2 tsp red wine vinegar
1 tbsp chopped parsley
salt and freshly ground
   black pepper

This recipe is guaranteed to make the whole family happy. It's packed full of flavour and ready in under an hour.

Fry the onion in a little oil in a pan until it's soft and translucent, then add the cinnamon and cumin and stir for 1 minute. Cool, then add half of the mixture to the mince along with 2 tablespoons of the pine nuts and season well.

Divide the mixture into 24 and roll each lump into a neat ball between your hands. Fry them in a little oil until they brown all over (you might need to do this in batches). Lift them into a colander to drain while you make the sauce.

Put the rest of the onion mix into the frying pan (tip out any excess oil first), and add the tomatoes, sugar and vinegar. Bubble gently for 5 minutes, then add the koftas. Cook for 15 minutes, turning the koftas halfway through cooking. Make sure they are cooked through, then serve scattered with the remaining pine nuts and the parsley.

Per serving 386 kcals, **protein** 27.8g, **carbohydrate** 8.2g, **fat** 26.5g, **saturated fat** 8.5g, **fibre** 2.1g, **salt** 0.3g

Creamy lamb and tomato curry

1½ hours | serves 4 | easy

2 tbsp olive oil

1 large onion, halved
 and sliced

3 garlic cloves, crushed

small chunk of fresh
 root ginger, peeled and
 finely grated

2 tbsp tomato purée

2 tsp garam masala

2 tsp ground cumin

2 tsp turmeric

½ tsp ground coriander

1 tsp mild chilli powder

5 cardamom pods,
 seeds ground

500g lamb neck fillet,
 cut into chunks

300ml chicken stock

2 tbsp ground almonds

4 tomatoes, chopped

6 tbsp natural yoghurt

cooked rice or bread,
 to serve

This creamy curry recipe takes a little longer to cook than the average curry, but it's totally worth it and it's really easy. Big flavours, minimal effort – it's a winner for us!

Heat the oil in a pan. Cook the onion, garlic and ginger until the onion is very soft and has a little colour. Add the tomato purée and all the spices and cook for 2–3 minutes. Add the lamb, cooking and turning it in the mix for a few minutes until the lamb is opaque. Add the chicken stock, bring to a simmer, cover and cook for 1 hour.

Add the almonds and tomatoes and cook for another 15 minutes, uncovered. Stir in the yoghurt and heat gently, then serve the curry with rice or bread.

Per serving 451 kcals, **protein** 33.5g, **carbohydrate** 14g, **fat** 28.3g, **saturated fat** 9.5g, **fibre** 2.8g, **salt** 0.6g

Meatballs with tomato and green olive sauce

45 minutes | serves 4 | easy

500g lean pork mince
1 small red onion, grated
   or very finely chopped
pinch of dried chilli flakes
½ tsp fennel seeds, crushed
   in a pestle and mortar
4 tbsp grated Parmesan
1 tbsp olive oil
300g cooked buttered
   tagliatelle, to serve
salt and freshly ground
   black pepper

For the tomato and olive sauce

2 tbsp olive oil
3 garlic cloves, sliced
2 x 400g cans plum
   tomatoes
4 cloves
12 green olives, pitted
   and quartered
small bunch of basil leaves,
   shredded

Meatballs are a great family and budget choice and can be made ahead and frozen. These easy pork meatballs are cooked in a rich tomato, garlic and olive sauce. Serve with pasta, rice or mash.

To make the sauce, heat the oil in a pan. Add the garlic and sizzle gently for a couple of minutes. Tip in the tomatoes and cloves, then simmer for 15 minutes until the sauce has thickened a little, squashing down the tomatoes as they cook.

Meanwhile, to make the meatballs, put the rest of the ingredients in a bowl, except the oil and tagliatelle, season and mix well with your hands. Form into walnut-sized balls (you'll get about 20). Heat a frying pan with the oil. Brown the meatballs all over – do this in batches to avoid overcrowding the pan.

Scoop the cloves out of the tomato sauce, then add the meatballs and olives. Simmer for another 20 minutes. Stir in the basil to finish. Serve with buttered tagliatelle.

Per serving 641 kcals, **protein** 45.5g, **carbohydrate** 65.9g, **fat** 24g, **saturated fat** 8.5g, **fibre** 4.2g, **salt** 1.24g

Peppers baked with lamb and rice

1 hour 20 minutes | serves 4 | easy

400g lean lamb mince

1 tbsp olive oil

1 large onion, sliced

2 garlic cloves, sliced

½ tsp ground cinnamon

½ tsp ground cumin

½ tsp dried oregano

pinch of chilli flakes
   (optional)

150g cooked basmati
   rice (use a pack of
   microwaveable rice or
   cook 75g rice and cool)

1 tbsp tomato purée

200ml chicken stock

2 tbsp chopped flat-leaf
   parsley

4 tbsp pine nuts

4 green, yellow or red
   peppers

salt and freshly ground
   black pepper

Stuffed peppers make an easy, healthy all-in-one meal.

Preheat the oven to 200°C/Fan 180°C/Gas 6. Cook the lamb in the oil in a non-stick pan until browned. Add the onion and garlic and cook until soft. Stir in the cinnamon, cumin, oregano and chilli flakes, if using.

Add the cooked rice and tomato purée, then pour in half the chicken stock. Stir in the parsley and pine nuts and season. Cut the tops off the peppers, remove the seeds and membrane inside and cut the peppers in half. Spoon the lamb and rice mix into the peppers, then sit them in the pan or a separate baking dish, pour round the rest of stock, cover with foil and bake for 45 minutes. Take off the foil and cook for another 10 minutes or until the peppers are tender.

Per serving 388 kcals, **protein** 24g, **carbohydrate** 24.1g, **fat** 22.4g, **saturated fat** 7.1g, **fibre** 3.5g, **salt** 0.66g

Lamb rogan josh

1 hour 45 minutes, plus marinating | serves 6 | easy

2 garlic cloves, crushed

2 tsp finely grated fresh
   root ginger

1½ tsp mild chilli powder

700g lamb neck fillet,
   cut into chunks

2 onions, roughly chopped

2 tbsp groundnut oil

1 cinnamon stick

6 cardamom pods,
   squashed

4 cloves, ground

1 tsp ground cumin

2 tsp ground coriander

1 tsp paprika (not smoked)

2 bay leaves

1½ tbsp tomato purée

450ml light chicken stock

100g full-fat natural
   yoghurt

few leaves of coriander,
   chopped, to garnish

rice and Indian breads,
   to serve

salt

This is an easy, one pot lamb rogan josh that is sure to be a family favourite. Cook and eat it now, or freeze ahead for a stress-free weekday meal.

Combine the garlic, ginger and chilli powder and toss with the lamb. Chill for a couple of hours or overnight, if you prefer.

Put the onions in a small food processor with a splash of water and whizz to a purée. Heat the oil in a large pan with a lid. Add the cinnamon and cardamom and cook for 2 minutes. Add the onion purée with a large pinch of salt and cook for 4–5 minutes until the paste thickens.

Add the rest of the spices and the bay leaves, cook for 1 minute, then add the marinated lamb and cook until opaque and browned. Add the tomato purée and stock and bring to a simmer. Put on a lid and simmer for 1½ hours or until the lamb is tender.

Add the yoghurt and simmer for 5 minutes. Scatter with coriander and serve with some rice and breads alongside.

Per serving 344 kcals, **protein** 24.2g, **carbohydrate** 7.5g, **fat** 23.9g, **saturated fat** 9.5g, **fibre** 1.4g, **salt** 0.5g

Lamb hotpot with swede topping

2 hours 10 minutes | serves 6 | easy

1kg best end of neck or
   diced stewing lamb
oil, for frying
2 onions, chopped
2 carrots, peeled and
   chopped
2 bay leaves
2 tbsp plain flour
500ml lamb stock
dash of Worcestershire
   sauce
1 swede, peeled, quartered
   and thinly sliced
butter, for dotting over
chopped parsley, to serve
salt and freshly ground
   black pepper

This is a soupy recipe; the gravy produced is broth-like and there should be plenty to spoon over each serving. Topping this hotpot with swede instead of potato makes for a delicious twist on this British classic.

Brown the lamb in batches in a little oil in a deep ovenproof frying pan with a lid. Transfer to a bowl.

Brown the onions in a little more oil in the pan, followed by the carrots, then add these to the lamb. Tuck the bay leaves into the lamb mixture. Add the flour to the pan and stir for 2 minutes. Add the stock, bring to a boil and scrape the base well. Shake in the Worcestershire sauce and season.

Return the lamb and veg to the pan, put on a lid and cook for 1½ hours. Layer the swede on top, seasoning as you go, and dot butter over the top. Put the lid back on and cook for 20 minutes. Put under a preheated grill to brown up the top before serving, scattered with parsley.

Per serving 474 kcals, **protein** 33.8g, **carbohydrate** 15.2g, **fat** 31g, **saturated fat** 13.7g, **fibre** 4.3g, **salt** 0.3g

Simple Persian-style lamb stew

1½ hours | serves 4 | easy

750g lamb leg steaks or
   neck fillet, cut into
   chunks
oil, for frying
2 onions, chopped
2 tsp ground cinnamon
1 tsp ground cumin
3 cardamom pods,
   seeds crushed
1 tsp paprika
500ml chicken stock
1 tbsp tomato purée
100g dates, quartered
cooked basmati rice or
   couscous, to serve
pomegranate seeds and
   mint leaves, to serve

This Persian-inspired lamb stew is really simple and makes for a delicious, warming meal for the family. The pomegranate seeds and mint give it a lovely fresh flavour. If there are only two of you, freeze the rest for later.

Brown the lamb all over in a little oil in a frying pan, then add the onions and cook until golden and soft. Stir in all the spices and cook for 1 minute, then add the stock, tomato purée and dates. Cover and simmer gently for 1 hour or until the meat is tender.

Serve with basmati rice or couscous, scattered with the pomegranate seeds and mint leaves.

Per serving 500 kcals, **protein** 36.7g, **carbohydrate** 13.5g, **fat** 32.5g, **saturated fat** 14.9g, **fibre** 3.2g, **salt** 0.6g

Irish stew

2 hours 15 minutes | serves 6 | easy

1kg boneless lamb
   shoulder, well trimmed
   and cut into roughly
   3cm pieces
4 tbsp plain flour
knob of beef dripping or
   1 tbsp sunflower oil
15g butter, plus extra knob
2 medium onions, halved
   and thinly sliced
good grating of nutmeg
1 tbsp soft light brown
   sugar
2 x 440ml cans Irish stout,
   such as Guinness
1½ tbsp malt vinegar
4 medium carrots, peeled
   and thickly sliced
1 small swede, peeled
   and cut into roughly
   2cm cubes
4 medium potatoes,
   peeled and cut into
   roughly 2cm cubes
crusty bread, to serve
salt and freshly ground
   black pepper

A warming winter one pot of lamb shoulder slow-cooked in stout with swede and potatoes makes a wholesome family meal. It is also a good vehicle for serving up late-season lamb.

Preheat the oven to 180°C/Fan 160°C/Gas 4. Put the lamb into a strong polythene food bag and sprinkle in the flour along with some salt. Close the bag and shake the lamb until coated with the flour.

Melt the dripping or oil and knob of butter in a large casserole and fry the lamb in 2 batches until nicely browned on all sides. As soon as each batch is browned, transfer to a plate. You may need to add a little extra fat to the pan for the last batch.

Melt the 15g butter in the same pan and add the onions. Season with lots of black pepper, then cook over a medium heat for about 5 minutes or until very soft and lightly browned, stirring often. Sprinkle over the nutmeg and stir in the sugar. Tip in the meat, pour over the stout and vinegar, then add the carrots, swede and potatoes. Add just enough cold water to cover, around 400ml, and bring to the boil. Skim off any foam that forms on the surface. Remove the pan from the hob, cover with a lid and cook in the centre of the oven for 1 hour 10 minutes.

Remove the lid and return to the oven for a further 20 minutes. This will reduce the sauce a little. Ladle into deep, warmed plates and serve with bread – greens have no place here.

Per serving 479 kcals, **protein** 37.8g, **carbohydrate** 33.4g, **fat** 18.7g, **saturated fat** 9.1g, **fibre** 4.8g, **salt** 0.45g

Slow-cooked lamb with spring veg and fresh mint sauce

4 hours | serves 6 | easy

1 leg of lamb (2–2½kg)
oil, for coating and frying
300g small round shallots,
    peeled
large glass of white wine
200ml chicken stock
300g baby leeks
300g peas
300g broad beans,
    double-podded

For the mint sauce

large bunch of mint, leaves
    picked and chopped
1½ tbsp golden caster
    sugar
5 tbsp white wine vinegar

The best roast lamb to share with the family. Spring veg goes so well with new-season lamb, but if fresh veg is not in season, frozen will work just as well. If you have some mint to hand, the homemade mint sauce is quick and easy and makes the best accompaniment to the lamb, along with buttered new potatoes.

Preheat the oven to 160°C/Fan 140°C/Gas 3. Rub the lamb with oil then brown really well all over in a shallow casserole or solid roasting tin. Once the lamb is browned, take it out and cook the shallots in the same pan until golden (use a little more oil if you need to). Put the lamb and shallots back into the casserole or roasting tin and pour in the wine and stock. Cover with a lid or a double sheet of foil then put in the oven for 3 hours.

Add the leeks to the casserole and cook for another 20–25 minutes or until tender. Add the peas and broad beans, cover again then give it another 10–15 minutes until hot.

To make the sauce, put the mint leaves in a bowl with the sugar and pour over 5 tablespoons of boiling water. Leave to cool then stir in the vinegar. Serve the lamb and veg with the mint sauce.

Per serving 571 kcals, **protein** 58.8g, **carbohydrate** 19.1g, **fat** 26.5g, **saturated fat** 11.7g, **fibre** 7.8g, **salt** 0.4g

Leg of lamb with pomegranate and balsamic onions

2½ hours | serves 4-6 | easy

4 large red onions, peeled
   and sliced 1cm thick
2 sprigs of rosemary
6 garlic cloves
1 leg of lamb (about 2kg)
3 tbsp olive oil, plus extra
   to drizzle
2 tbsp pomegranate
   molasses
1 tsp harissa
4 tbsp balsamic vinegar
20 mint leaves
wild garlic wilted in butter,
   or other greens, to serve
   (optional)
salt and freshly ground
   black pepper

The sweetness of the roasted onions is offset by a good splash of balsamic vinegar, and pomegranate molasses is used with a touch of harissa as a glaze for the lamb.

Preheat the oven to 200°C/Fan 180°C/Gas 6. Lay out the red onions evenly in a roasting tin with the rosemary and garlic scattered around. Season the lamb leg all over and sit it on top. Drizzle over the olive oil and roast in the oven for about 1 hour 20 minutes, if you like your lamb pink, turning the meat over halfway through. (If you are using a meat thermometer, 60°C will give you pink lamb.)

Mix the pomegranate molasses and harissa together in a small bowl. Spread over the lamb after it's had its cooking time, then put the meat back in the oven for 10 minutes to glaze. Take it out and put it on a plate to rest.

Scoop out the red onions, rosemary and garlic along with any juice from the tin and put in the same bowl. Mix in the balsamic vinegar and mint leaves and taste for seasoning. Add another small drizzle of olive oil.

Serve the lamb with the onions and wild garlic or other greens, if you like.

Per serving (4) 537 kcals, **protein** 49.7g, **carbohydrate** 16g, **fat** 29.7g, **saturated fat** 10.3g, **fibre** 3.3g, **salt** 0.3g

Slow-braised lamb shanks with coconut and cardamom

2½ hours | serves 2 | easy

2 tbsp vegetable oil

4 cardamom pods, bashed

3 cloves, ground

½ tsp ground cinnamon

1 tsp chilli powder

3 tsp ground coriander

1 onion, finely sliced

2 small lamb shanks

large chunk of fresh root
    ginger, peeled and grated

3 garlic cloves, crushed

400g can coconut milk

about 750ml chicken stock

1 tsp garam masala

cooked basmati rice,
    to serve

small bunch of coriander,
    chopped, to serve

salt

This recipe makes for delicious, fall-off-the-bone meat in a flavour-packed, lightly spiced sauce. It's perfect for a special meal for two.

Heat the oil in a casserole large enough to fit the meat in a single layer. Add the spices and cook for 20 seconds until sizzling. Add the onion with a pinch of salt and cook until softened and browned at the edges.

Add the lamb to the onions and stir to brown a little on all sides. Add the ginger and garlic and cook for a few minutes, stirring. Add the coconut milk and enough stock to come three-quarters of the way up the lamb. Cover and simmer for 2 hours or until tender.

Take out the lamb carefully, add the garam masala to the casserole and reduce the liquid until saucy. Put the lamb back to warm through, remove the cardamom pods, then serve with basmati rice, sprinkled with coriander.

Per serving 915 kcals, **protein** 53.1g, **carbohydrate** 16.5g, **fat** 71.3g, **saturated fat** 41.4g, **fibre** 2.8g, **salt** 0.6g

Mustard mac 'n' cheese with pastrami and crumbs

50 minutes | serves 4 | easy

800ml semi-skimmed milk

1 bunch of spring onions, whites and greens separated, whites halved lengthways, greens sliced

300g macaroni

50g butter

60g plain flour

25g Parmesan, finely grated

200g hard cheeses, grated (Cheddar and Gruyère are great)

1 tbsp English mustard

100g pastrami, cut into strips

4 heaped tbsp dried breadcrumbs

salt and freshly ground black pepper

A fun twist on the American classic mac 'n' cheese. Pastrami and spring onions are baked with the macaroni and the dish is finished with a crunchy, golden breadcrumb topping.

Put the milk and spring onion whites in a pan together. Bring the milk to just below boiling point, then turn off the heat and leave to infuse while you cook the pasta.

Cook the macaroni until al dente, then drain well and set aside. Melt the butter in the same pan used to cook the macaroni. Stir in the flour to make a smooth paste and cook for a couple of minutes. Strain out and discard the onion from the milk, then very gradually stir the milk into the flour and butter until you get a smooth sauce. Bring to a gentle simmer and cook for a few minutes until nicely thickened, then take off the heat and stir in half the Parmesan, the other cheeses, the mustard and some seasoning.

Stir in the macaroni, pastrami and spring onion greens and tip everything into an ovenproof dish. Scatter with the remaining Parmesan and breadcrumbs, plus a little more salt. When you're ready, place the dish under the grill until the topping is golden, crunchy and piping hot.

Per serving 859 kcals, **protein** 41.5g, **carbohydrate** 90.3g, **fat** 36g, **saturated fat** 21.2g, **fibre** 4.1g, **salt** 2.9g

Chilli con carne

2 hours | serves 4 | easy

1 large onion

2 large garlic cloves, crushed

1 tbsp olive oil

500g good-quality or aged beef mince

3 tsp chipotle powder or paste

2 tsp ground cumin

1 tsp ground coriander

¼ tsp cayenne pepper

½ tsp dried oregano

1 tbsp tomato purée

400g can chopped tomatoes

250ml red wine

20g dark chocolate (70% cocoa solids), broken into chunks

4 semi-dried tomatoes, chopped

2 x 400g cans kidney beans, drained and rinsed

1 vegetable stock cube

1 red pepper, deseeded and cut into chunks (optional)

salt and freshly ground black pepper

Our most popular chilli con carne recipe *ever*! Made Tex-Mex style with aged minced beef, chipotle powder, red wine, 70% dark chocolate and semi-dried tomatoes. The texture of good-quality beef mince goes perfectly with the kidney beans. Enjoy alongside rice or corn tortillas, lettuce, avocado, fresh coriander and Tabasco.

Preheat the oven to 180°C/Fan 160°C/Gas 4. Gently fry the onion and garlic in the oil in a casserole. Turn up the heat, add the mince and fry until evenly browned and you have a light crust on the bottom of the pan. Add the chipotle, spices and dried oregano, then cook for 1 minute until the meat is well coated.

Add the tomato purée, chopped tomatoes, wine, chocolate, semi-dried tomatoes and kidney beans and crumble in the stock cube. (You can use less or no wine if you prefer, just use water instead, plus a small splash of vinegar or lemon juice.) Put it in the oven with a lid for at least 1 hour 30 minutes. Add the pepper (if using) for the last 30 minutes – you may need to add a touch of water at this stage as well.

Season and serve with whichever accompaniments you prefer.

Per serving 589 kcals, **protein** 34.5g, **carbohydrate** 25g, **fat** 32g, **saturated fat** 11g, **fibre** 9g, **salt** 2.3g

Diner-style chilli

1 hour | serves 4 | easy

500g beef mince

2 onions, chopped

2 tbsp mild chilli powder

1 tbsp dried oregano

2 tsp garlic powder or
    granules

2 tsp ground cumin

4 tbsp tomato purée

500ml passata

2 tbsp pickled jalapeños,
    chopped

300ml chicken stock

400g can kidney beans,
    drained and rinsed

salt and freshly ground
    black pepper

To serve

grated Cheddar, extra
    jalapeños, soured cream,
    tortilla chips

This recipe is based on a simple US chilli that is served in bars and diners in small bowls or cups. This is also great served in burgers, hot dogs or over nachos.

Brown the mince all over in a hot non-stick pan (there should be enough fat released to fry the mince). Add the onions and cook until softened, then add the chilli powder, oregano and garlic powder and cumin. Fry for a few minutes, then tip in the tomato purée, passata and jalapeños. Add the chicken stock, then cover and simmer for 30 minutes. Add the kidney beans and cook for another 15 minutes, uncovered.

Season and serve in bowls with cheese, extra jalapeños, soured cream and tortilla chips.

Per serving 458 kcals, **protein** 35.2g, **carbohydrate** 24.5g, **fat** 22.4g, **saturated fat** 8.9g, **fibre** 8.6g, **salt** 1.6g

10-minute beef stroganoff

10 minutes | serves 2 | easy

150g pappardelle

250g sirloin steak,
    trimmed of all fat

1 tbsp groundnut oil

100g baby chestnut
    mushrooms, sliced

knob of butter

1 garlic clove, crushed

2 tsp sweet smoked
    paprika

100g soured cream

splash of chicken stock

handful of flat-leaf parsley,
    chopped

salt and freshly ground
    black pepper

Beef stroganoff is always comforting. This version is super quick and easy – on the table in just 10 minutes – so it's perfect if there's just two of you. If you usually serve this with rice, try it with pappardelle as here, instead.

Cook the pappardelle. Meanwhile, slice the steak into thin strips and season.

Heat the oil in a large frying pan until very hot, then quickly sear the beef until browned on both sides. (Do this in batches if you need to and don't overcrowd the pan.) Scoop out the meat and keep it warm under foil.

Put the mushrooms into the same pan with the butter, cook until soft, then tip in the garlic and paprika and fry for a couple of minutes.

Add back the beef with the soured cream and stock and let everything bubble up. Stir through the parsley, then serve spooned onto the pasta.

Per serving 578 kcals, **protein** 39.2g, **carbohydrate** 43g, **fat** 27.5g, **saturated fat** 11.9g, **fibre** 1.1g, **salt** 1.6g

Beef paprikash

3 hours | serves 4 | easy

500g braising beef

1 tbsp plain flour, seasoned really well

1 tbsp olive oil

1 large onion, halved and sliced

2 garlic cloves, crushed

250g chestnut mushrooms, halved if large

1 red pepper, deseeded and sliced

1 tbsp paprika

2 tsp caraway seeds

400g can chopped tomatoes

300ml beef stock

small bunch of parsley, chopped

crusty bread or cooked basmati rice, to serve

soured cream, to serve

salt and freshly ground black pepper

Paprikash or paprika beef is a popular Hungarian dish. You can also try making this with chicken, if you like.

Preheat the oven to 180°C/Fan 160°C/Gas 4. Toss the beef with the seasoned flour then brown all over in the oil in a large pan. Scoop out, then add the onion to the pan and cook well until soft and browned at the edges. Add the garlic, mushrooms and pepper and cook for 5 minutes until softened.

Return the beef to the pan and add the spices, tomatoes and beef stock. Put on a lid, transfer to the oven and cook for 2–2½ hours until the beef is really tender and the sauce has thickened. Stir in the parsley.

Serve with crusty bread or rice and soured cream.

Per serving 314 kcals, **protein** 32g, **carbohydrate** 13.4g, **fat** 15.1g, **saturated fat** 5.1g, **fibre** 3.2g, **salt** 1.15g

Slow-braised Korean short ribs

4½ hours, plus overnight chilling | serves 4 | easy

2 tbsp oil

8 single beef short ribs,
  each about 8cm long

bunch of spring onions,
  finely chopped

4 garlic cloves, crushed

3cm piece fresh root
  ginger, peeled and finely
  grated

4 tbsp rice wine vinegar

juice of 1 lime

3 tbsp gochujang

2 tbsp soy sauce

4 tbsp soft brown sugar

1 tbsp sesame oil

1 tbsp sesame seeds,
  ground in a pestle
  and mortar

750ml water

cooked basmati rice,
  to serve

For the pickles

4 tbsp rice wine vinegar

2 tbsp sesame oil

2 tsp golden caster sugar

½ red chilli, finely diced

1 garlic clove, halved

2 small ridge cucumbers,
  or use ½ a normal

Gochujang is a Korean paste made from hot red peppers and fermented soy beans, which gives a savoury, spicy, umami depth to sauces. Buy it in Asian supermarkets or online.

Preheat the oven to 160°C/Fan 140°C/Gas 3. Heat the oil in a large non-stick frying pan then brown the ribs in batches, getting a good dark colour and rendering down as much fat as you can. Pour away the fat as you cook.

Put the spring onions, garlic and ginger in a large ovenproof pot with a lid where the ribs will sit in a single layer. Add the rest of the ingredients, cover, then cook in the oven for 4 hours.

Carefully remove the ribs, then cool. Chill the cooking liquid until the fat settles and hardens on top. If you can do this the day before, great; if not, start in the morning and a couple of hours in the fridge should do it.

To make the pickles, combine the vinegar, oil, sugar, chilli and garlic. Cut some strips of skin from the cucumber using a peeler then cut the cucumber into discs. Toss with the liquid and chill (remove the garlic before serving).

When the fat has solidified, scoop it off the top and discard. Put the pot back on the heat and simmer the sauce, if you want to thicken it. Add the ribs and cook, turning in the liquid until heated. Serve with the rice and pickles.

Per serving 717 kcals, **protein** 34.9g, **carbohydrate** 29.2g, **fat** 50.6g, **saturated fat** 17.3g, **fibre** 3g, **salt** 2.1g

Vietnamese beef and lemongrass one pot

2 hours | serves 6 | easy

1 tsp oil

600g lean steak, diced

4 shallots, sliced

3 lemongrass stalks, woody
   leaves removed, 2 finely
   chopped, 1 bashed but
   left whole

2 garlic cloves, crushed

2 red chillies, chopped

3 kaffir lime leaves

2 star anise

400ml vegetable stock

1 tbsp fish sauce,
   plus extra to season
   (optional)

juice of 1 lime, plus
   wedges to serve

coriander leaves, to serve

cooked jasmine rice and
   Asian greens, to serve

salt and freshly ground
   black pepper

We love Vietnamese-inspired flavours, and this Vietnamese beef and lemongrass one pot is a definite winner. There's minimal washing up, it's under 200 calories, but still packs a punch in terms of flavour.

Preheat the oven to 160°C/Fan 140°C/Gas 3. Heat the oil in an ovenproof pan with a lid. Season the steak pieces and fry in batches, scooping out once browned. Add the shallots, lemongrass, garlic and chillies to the same pan and cook until fragrant. Add the lime leaves and star anise and return the meat to the pan, then cover with the stock. Add the fish sauce, put the lid on and transfer to the oven to cook for 1½ hours. (Remove the lid for the last 15 minutes to thicken the sauce if it's too thin.)

Add the lime juice and season with more fish sauce, if you like. Scatter with coriander and serve in bowls with jasmine rice and Asian greens.

Per serving 155 kcals, **protein** 21.6g, **carbohydrate** 2.1g, **fat** 6.5g, **saturated fat** 2.6g, **fibre** 0.7g, **salt** 0.8g

Beef, red wine and black olive stew

3 hours | serves 4 | easy

600g braising beef
  (chuck or shin), in chunks
groundnut oil, for frying
12 small shallots, peeled
100g smoked streaky
  bacon, diced
1 tbsp plain flour
200ml red wine
200ml beef stock
12 pitted black olives
1kg Maris Piper potatoes,
  peeled and halved
25g butter
dash of milk
small handful of parsley,
  chopped (optional)
salt and freshly ground
  black pepper

If you get your beef from the butcher you'll be able to ask for specific cuts such as chuck and shin, which are great for stews and braising.

Season the beef then brown in batches in a large casserole with a little oil. Scoop out each batch as it becomes browned then add the shallots to the pan, brown all over and remove. Add the bacon and cook until golden, then return the beef and shallots to the pan. Sprinkle over the flour and stir until it disappears. Slowly add the wine then the stock, stirring. Put on a lid and bring to a simmer, then cook for 2 hours.

Take off the lid, add the olives and cook for another 30 minutes.

Meanwhile, boil the potatoes until tender then mash with the butter and a little milk. Season and serve with the stew and a sprinkle of parsley, if using.

Per serving 748 kcals, **protein** 62.6g, **carbohydrate** 45.9g, **fat** 30.9g, **saturated fat** 12.4g, **fibre** 4.3g, **salt** 2.3g

Tuscan slow-cooked shin of beef with Chianti

5 hours | serves 6–8 | easy

600g beef shin,
   off the bone, diced
olive oil, for frying
2 large onions,
   finely chopped
3 celery sticks,
   finely chopped
1 carrot, peeled and
   finely diced
6 fat garlic cloves,
   finely chopped
750ml Chianti or other
   robust red wine
4 tbsp tomato purée
4 bay leaves
150ml beef stock
salt and freshly ground
   black pepper

Italian cuisine never goes out of fashion. This is a brilliant example of how to do things simply but perfectly. It does take a while to cook, but it requires very little actual hands-on time. Serve with pappardelle pasta or potatoes.

Preheat the oven to 180°C/Fan 160°C/Gas 4. Season the meat, then brown it all over in a large casserole with a little oil. Take out then cook the onions, celery, carrot and garlic until softened, adding a little more oil if you need to. Pour in the wine, let it bubble up, then stir in the tomato purée, bay leaves and the beef stock. Add the beef back to the pan and bring to a simmer.

Cover with a lid and put in the oven. Cook for 4 hours until the meat starts to fall apart. Pull the meat into chunks and stir through the sauce.

Per serving (6) 335 kcals, **protein** 24.1g, **carbohydrate** 9.7g, **fat** 12.3g, **saturated fat** 4g, **fibre** 3g, **salt** 0.3g

Cantonese braised turnips with short ribs

3 hours 40 minutes, plus overnight chilling | serves 6 | easy

2.5kg beef short ribs,
  in single-bone sections
250ml light soy sauce
250ml cider
4 garlic cloves, sliced
4 spring onions, sliced
2 star anise
1 orange, zest removed
  with a potato peeler
2 tsp toasted sesame oil
2 carrots, peeled and sliced
4 small turnips, halved

This is a complete meal in one, but if you're really hungry, add some roast potatoes, too.

Preheat the oven to 220°C/Fan 200°C/Gas 7. Put the ribs in a roasting tin, combine the soy sauce, cider and garlic and pour over the ribs. Add the spring onions, star anise and orange zest, then the sesame oil, carrots and turnips. Cover with foil and put in the oven.

Lower the oven temperature to 160°C/Fan 140°C/Gas 4. Cook for 2 hours, covered (or until very tender), then cook for a further 30 minutes, uncovered, to reduce the sauce a little. Skim off any fat on the surface or cool then chill overnight so that the excess fat sets and can be easily removed.

Reheat in an oven preheated to 180°C/Fan 160°C/Gas 4 for 40 minutes until piping hot.

Per serving 771 kcals, **protein** 69.9g, **carbohydrate** 11.2g, **fat** 48.4g, **saturated fat** 21.4g, **fibre** 3.1ga, **salt** 5g

Rib of beef roasted over potatoes

2 hours | serves 8 | easy

rib of beef (about 3kg)

½ tbsp English mustard
   powder

2 tbsp plain flour

12 shallots, peeled

1.5kg potatoes, peeled and
   cut into large chunks
   (they need to fit under
   the rack)

150ml red wine

400ml beef stock

salt and freshly ground
   black pepper

This rib of beef makes a very easy Sunday roast. The potatoes are cooked in the beef's juices so they are extra delicious. Serve with a side of veggies.

Preheat the oven to 220°C/Fan 200°C/Gas 7. Rub the fat of the beef with the mustard powder and half the flour, then season well. Put the meat on a rack in a roasting tin. Roast the meat for 30 minutes, then turn the oven down to 160°C/Fan 140°C/Gas 3 and cook for another 15 minutes per 500g for medium-rare.

Around 30 minutes before the end of the beef cooking, take the tin out of the oven and lift out the beef and rack. Add the shallots and potatoes to the roasting tin and stir them around in the beef fat. Season well. Put the beef and rack back in the tin over the veggies and continue to cook for 30 minutes.

Lift out the beef and rack and set aside on a plate to rest, covered in foil. Stir the potatoes, turn the oven up to 220°C/Fan 200°C/Gas 7 and cook them at the top of the oven for another 15 minutes or until crisp.

When the potatoes are done, lift them out of the tin and keep them warm in the oven. Pour off any oil, then squash the shallots in the tin. Stir in the remaining flour, then put the tin over a low heat. Add the wine and stock, stir and bubble everything together. Cook for 10 minutes, then strain the gravy and season it if it needs it. When you carve the beef, add any juices to the gravy. Serve with the roasted potatoes.

Per serving 818 kcals, **protein** 66.4g, **carbohydrate** 35.6g, **fat** 43.1g, **saturated fat** 19.1g, **fibre** 19.1g, **salt** 0.6g

Fish and seafood

Corn, chive and prawn chowder

15 minutes | serves 4 | easy

2 corn cobs, husks
   removed and kernels
   cut off
4 spring onions, sliced
1 large potato, peeled
   and diced
knob of butter
750ml light fresh chicken
   stock, or make up with
   a cube or concentrate
4 tbsp double cream
150g North Atlantic
   prawns, peeled
small bunch of chives,
   snipped
salt and freshly ground
   black pepper

There's nothing more hearty and satisfying than a bowl of thick, hot, corn chowder. This version has added chives and prawns and is so simple to make – you just need one pot and the soup will be ready to eat in less than 15 minutes!

Cook the corn kernels, spring onions and potato gently in the butter in a pan for 2 minutes. Add the stock and simmer for 8–10 minutes until the potato and corn are tender.

Stir in the cream and prawns, season, and simmer until the prawns are just heated through. Stir in the chives and serve.

Per serving 248 kcals, **protein** 16.8g, **carbohydrate** 19.8g, **fat** 12g, **saturated fat** 5.6g, **fibre** 1.9g, **salt** 1.35g

Cheat's seafood stew

40 minutes | serves 3 | easy

1 onion, halved and sliced
1 tbsp olive oil
pinch of saffron
300g baby new potatoes,
  peeled and halved
500ml chicken stock
2 plum tomatoes,
  roughly chopped
300–400g frozen seafood
  mix (we used a mix of
  prawns, scallops, squid
  and mussels)
handful of flat-leaf parsley,
  roughly chopped
3 tbsp mayonnaise
½ garlic clove, crushed
pinch of smoked paprika
6 baguette slices, toasted
salt and freshly ground
  black pepper

Seafood stew doesn't have to take hours to make. This cheat's recipe is packed full of those delicious fish flavours but is on the table in under an hour, so it's still achievable midweek.

Cook the onion in the oil in a pan until soft. Stir in the saffron and new potatoes then add the chicken stock and tomatoes. Simmer gently for about 15 minutes, or until the potatoes are tender, then add the seafood mix and simmer until cooked through. Stir in the parsley and season.

Mix the mayonnaise with the garlic and smoked paprika. Serve the stew with the baguette toasts and mayonnaise.

Per serving 505 kcals, **protein** 30.1g, **carbohydrate** 50.6g, **fat** 18.8g, **saturated fat** 3.2g, **fibre** 6.5g, **salt** 2.6g

Mussel and tomato chowder

45 minutes | serves 4 | easy

400ml fish or chicken stock
1kg mussels, cleaned
olive oil, for frying and
  to serve
1 large potato,
  peeled and cubed
1 onion, finely chopped
2 garlic cloves, crushed
1 bay leaf
sprig of thyme
200ml white wine
300g cherry tomatoes
small bunch of parsley,
  roughly chopped
Tabasco, to season
salt and freshly ground
  black pepper

Clean mussels by rinsing them, pulling off any beards and throwing away any that won't close when tapped on the sink.

Bring the stock to a simmer in a large pan and tip in the mussels. Cover and cook for 2–3 minutes or until all the mussels open. Drain, reserving the liquid, and discard any mussels that haven't opened.

Put a little oil in the pan and add the potato and onion. Stir and fry for a few minutes until the onion softens. Add the garlic, herbs and white wine. Simmer for 1 minute, strain in the mussel cooking liquid through a fine sieve (hold back any grit) and simmer until the potato softens, then add the tomatoes and parsley and simmer until the tomatoes start to burst.

Pull most of the mussels from the shells and put them back into the chowder, season well, then add the remaining mussels with their shells. Season with Tabasco and a swirl of olive oil.

Per serving 195 kcals, **protein** 16.8g, **carbohydrate** 17g, **fat** 3.1g, **saturated fat** 0.5g, **fibre** 3.6g, **salt** 0.9g

Spicy crab and sweetcorn chowder with avocado

35 minutes | serves 6 | easy

2 tbsp olive oil

1 onion, finely chopped

450g potatoes, peeled and cut into little cubes

1.5 litres chicken stock

4 spring onions, 2 halved and 2 finely sliced

a few coriander stalks and a handful of roughly chopped leaves

½ celery stick, cut into thin batons

2 x 340g cans sweetcorn, drained

2 cans white crab meat, drained

2 avocados, peeled, stoned and thickly sliced

1–2 red chillies, shredded

170ml soured cream

2 limes, cut into wedges

salt and freshly ground black pepper

Use crab meat in this spicy chowder packed with delicious fresh ingredients and zingy lime and avocado. Tinned crab works really well in cooked dishes and is a fraction of the price of fresh.

Heat the oil in a large saucepan. Tip in the onion and cook for 8 minutes or until soft. Add the potatoes and cook for 3 minutes more. Pour over the stock.

Tie the halved spring onions, coriander stalks and celery into a little bundle with some cooking string. Drop this into the saucepan and simmer for 15 minutes, or until the potatoes are tender.

Remove the bundle and add the sweetcorn and crab meat. Stir and heat through. Season, then add the chopped coriander leaves. Spoon into bowls and add the sliced avocado, shredded chilli, a dollop of soured cream and the sliced spring onions. Serve with a squeeze of lime.

Per serving 497 kcals, **protein** 31g, **carbohydrate** 41.8g, **fat** 23.6g, **saturated fat** 7.2g, **fibre** 6g, **salt** 1.4g

Fish curry with tomatoes and tamarind

30 minutes | serves 4 | easy

1 onion, quartered

2 garlic cloves, peeled

2cm piece fresh root
  ginger, peeled and
  roughly chopped

1 red chilli, roughly
  chopped

bunch of coriander, leaves
  separated from stems

1 tbsp oil

1 tsp black mustard seeds

small handful of curry
  leaves (optional)

½ tsp turmeric

1 tsp ground coriander

1 tsp ground cumin

400g plum tomatoes,
  diced

2 tbsp tamarind paste

200ml water

500g sustainable firm
  white fish fillets (such as
  hake or pollack), skinned
  and cut into 4cm cubes

cooked basmati rice,
  to serve

This fish curry is a super-easy recipe – ready in 30 minutes and under 300 calories per serving, it's packed with fantastic flavours.

Whizz the onion, garlic, ginger, chilli and the coriander stems in a blender until they form a paste.

Heat the oil in a pan and fry the black mustard seeds and curry leaves, if using, until fragrant. Add the paste and fry for 2 minutes, then add the turmeric, coriander and cumin. Fry for 2 minutes more then add the tomatoes and the tamarind paste with the water and cook until the tomatoes start to break down.

Stir in the fish, cover and simmer for 5 minutes until cooked. Serve with rice.

Per serving 206 kcals, **protein** 24.8g, **carbohydrate** 11g, **fat** 6.5g, **saturated fat** 0.9g, **fibre** 2.1g, **salt** 0.4g

Spanish prawns, peppers and aioli

45 minutes | serves 2 | easy

2 peppers, 1 red and
  1 yellow, deseeded and
  cut into large chunks
1½ lemons, 1 quartered,
  ½ juiced
4 large garlic cloves,
  3 unpeeled, 1 thinly
  sliced
200g small cooking
  chorizo sausages, halved
1 onion, cut into 8 chunks
1½ tbsp olive oil
1 tbsp sherry vinegar
2 tsp thyme leaves
2 tsp sweet smoked
  paprika
16 shell-on raw
  king prawns
150g mayonnaise
salt and freshly ground
  black pepper

Prawns, peppers and aioli make for a delicious Spanish-inspired one pot dinner for two. The garlicky aioli is a delicious side to dip the juicy prawns in.

Preheat the oven to 200°C/Fan 180°C/Gas 6. Toss together the peppers, lemon quarters, whole and sliced garlic, chorizo, onion, the olive oil, vinegar, thyme and 1½ teaspoons of the paprika with plenty of seasoning, and spread everything over a large roasting tray. Roast for 25 minutes, until the veg has begun to char and the sausages are cooked through.

Remove the whole garlic from the tray, add the prawns and put back in the oven, reserving the garlic. Roast for 5–10 minutes until the prawns are pink and crisp.

While the prawns are cooking, squeeze the roasted garlic out of its skins and mash well until smooth. Stir it through the mayonnaise with the remaining ½ teaspoon of paprika and the lemon juice.

Serve in a large dish, with a finger bowl on the side, and eat with plenty of the garlicky aioli.

Per serving 547 kcals, **protein** 18.4g, **carbohydrate** 12g, **fat** 46.4g, **saturated fat** 10g, **fibre** 2.5g, **salt** 2.2g

Linguine with samphire and prawns

20 minutes | serves 2 | easy

200g linguine

150g peeled, cooked tiger
or king prawns

150g samphire,
trimmed and blanched

grated zest and juice of
1 lemon

2 tbsp crème fraîche

The best recipe for samphire. This easy dish is made with linguine and pairs the sea vegetable samphire with tiger or king prawns in a super-quick pasta sauce.

Cook the pasta then drain, leaving a little water clinging to it. Tip it back into a pan and stir in the prawns, samphire, lemon zest and crème fraîche and cook until everything is heated through.

Season well with pepper (taste the samphire before adding any salt) and squeeze over enough lemon juice to taste.

Per serving 423 kcals, **protein** 26.5g, **carbohydrate** 54.6g, **fat** 11.3g, **saturated fat** 5.8g, **fibre** 4.1g, **salt** 2.7g

Saffron mussels with orzo and tomatoes

40 minutes | serves 2 | easy

1 tbsp olive oil

1 onion, finely chopped

1 celery stick,
  finely chopped

2 garlic cloves,
  finely chopped

200ml white wine

500ml fish or
  vegetable stock

2 pinches of saffron

350g plum tomatoes,
  diced

250g orzo

750g mussels, cleaned

75g crème fraîche

1 tbsp chopped dill

salt and freshly ground
  black pepper

A really easy one pot – it takes under an hour, looks fantastic and is packed full of delicious flavours. It's a great new way to make the most of mussels and tomatoes.

Heat the oil in a large, wide shallow pan with a lid. Add the onion, celery and garlic and gently soften for about 10 minutes. Stir in the wine, bring to the boil and bubble for 1 minute, then add the stock and saffron. Bring everything to the boil, stirring, then add the tomatoes and orzo and simmer for another 5 minutes until the orzo is about two-thirds cooked.

Tip in the mussels, cover and cook gently for 5 minutes, shaking the pan occasionally until the mussels have opened. Discard any mussels that don't open.

Stir in the crème fraîche and most of the dill with some seasoning – the mussels will add some saltiness themselves. Serve scattered with the remaining dill.

Per serving 677 kcals, **protein** 27.4g, **carbohydrate** 52.1g, **fat** 25.4g, **saturated fat** 11.8g, **fibre** 8.9g, **salt** 1.7g

Jansson's temptation

1 hour 10 minutes | serves 4 | easy

butter, for greasing
  and cooking
6 medium Desirée or Maris
  Piper potatoes, peeled
  and cut into matchsticks
2 Spanish onions, or 4
  small onions, finely sliced
1 can anchovy fillets,
  drained and chopped
284ml carton double
  cream
4 tbsp fresh breadcrumbs
freshly ground black
  pepper

This creamy, anchovy-spiked potato bake is a classic Swedish dish. Serve with crusty bread, salad or steamed greens.

Preheat the oven to 200°C/Fan 180°C/Gas 6. Butter a baking dish measuring about 20 x 30cm and layer in the potatoes, onions and anchovies, starting and finishing with a potato layer. Pour the cream over and dot with a little butter. Sprinkle on the breadcrumbs and a grinding of black pepper – don't add any salt as the anchovies are usually salty enough.

Cover with foil and bake for 20 minutes then take off the foil and bake for 25–35 minutes until the top has turned golden brown and the potatoes are soft when tested with the point of a knife. Serve piping hot.

Per serving 581 kcals, **protein** 9.9g, **carbohydrate** 38.5g, **fat** 44.1g, **saturated fat** 24.2g, **fibre** 4g, **salt** 1.11g

Prawn and dill pilaf

30 minutes | serves 2 | easy

30g butter

1 onion, halved and sliced

1 garlic clove, sliced

125g basmati rice

pinch of saffron

2 cloves

1 cinnamon stick

200ml chicken stock

150g cooked, peeled
   king prawns

½ bunch of dill, chopped

salt and freshly ground
   black pepper

This easy pilaf is full of flavour. Serve with a leafy side salad.

Melt the butter in a shallow pan with a lid. Cook the onion until really soft and golden. Add the garlic and cook for 1 minute. Stir in the rice and spices, then add the stock. Bring to a simmer, put on the lid and cook over a very gentle heat for 15 minutes, until all the stock has been absorbed and the rice is tender (add a splash of water if you need to).

Add the prawns, season, then cook for a couple of minutes to heat the prawns. Stir through the dill and serve.

Per serving 429 kcals, **protein** 23g, **carbohydrate** 56.1g, **fat** 14.1g, **saturated fat** 8g, **fibre** 2g, **salt** 2.38g

Spanish rice with saffron and mussels

45 minutes | serves 6 | easy

1 onion, chopped
2 cooking chorizo
  sausages, chopped
oil, for frying
500g bomba paella rice
400g can plum tomatoes,
  juice drained off
4 pieces roasted peppers
  from a jar, chopped
2 garlic cloves, sliced
1 tsp smoked paprika
pinch of saffron
1.25 litres chicken stock
1kg mussels, cleaned
salt and freshly ground
  black pepper

A spectacular crowd-pleasing dish, this paella uses chorizo, mussels and a pinch of saffron to pack in tons of flavour. Serve from a huge paella pan for extra impact.

Put the onion, chorizo and a little oil in a cold paella pan or very large, deep frying pan and turn on the heat. Fry gently until the chorizo releases some of its oil and the onion softens. Stir in the rice. Cook for 1 minute then add the tomatoes, peppers, garlic and paprika.

Season, add the saffron to the chicken stock and stir into the rice. Cook over a low heat, stirring every now and then. When the rice is almost done, stop stirring, level the top of the rice and add the mussels to the top. Put a lid on and cook for 2–3 minutes until the mussels open. Discard any mussels that don't open and serve immediately.

Per serving 446 kcals, **protein** 25.1g, **carbohydrate** 70.4g, **fat** 7.2g, **saturated fat** 2.5g, **fibre** 4.5g, **salt** 1.3g

Tuna, sweet potato and Gruyère melt

1 hour | serves 4 | easy

300ml double cream
100ml whole milk
2 x 120g cans tuna in
    spring water, drained
bunch of spring onions,
    chopped, including
    green bits
100g Gruyère, grated
750g sweet potatoes,
    peeled and cut into thin
    slices (you can use a
    mandoline or food
    processor)
green salad, to serve
salt and freshly ground
    black pepper

This tuna, sweet potato and Gruyère melt makes a really easy family meal. Just mix the ingredients in a baking dish and top with the sweet potato and cheese.

Preheat the oven to 180°C/Fan 160°C/Gas 6. Mix the cream, milk, tuna, onions and most of the cheese together. Layer up the sweet potato and tuna mix then season and scatter over the rest of the Gruyère. Bake for 40–50 minutes until bubbling and golden. Serve with a green salad.

Per serving 769 kcals, **protein** 21.4g, **carbohydrate** 52.9g, **fat** 50.5g, **saturated fat** 31.1g, **fibre** 8.7g, **salt** 0.9g

Confit salmon with lemon and parsley salsa

1 hour, plus cooling | serves 6 | easy

½ side salmon, skin on
   and pin-boned
10 black peppercorns
2 bay leaves
500–750ml olive oil
green salad, to serve
salt and freshly ground
   black pepper

For the salsa

2 lemons, plus wedges
   to serve
2 tbsp Dijon mustard
1 shallot, finely chopped
1 tsp golden caster sugar
4 tbsp olive oil
small bunch of parsley,
   chopped

Cooking salmon in olive oil gives it a silky texture and stops it from drying out.

Put the salmon in the snuggest ovenproof dish you can find. Add the peppercorns, a little salt, the bay leaves and enough olive oil to cover the fish completely and leave to sit for 10 minutes.

Preheat the oven to 140°C/Fan 120°C/Gas 2. Cover the dish with foil then bake the salmon for 30 minutes until the fish looks translucent and just cooked (if you have a meat thermometer, it should have reached 45°C in the thickest part of the fillet). Take it out of the oven then leave to cool completely in the oil. (It will keep cooking for a while in the oil.)

To make the salsa, cut the rind and pith off the lemons then cut in between the membrane to remove the segments. Chop the segments. Whisk the mustard, shallot and sugar together, squeezing in the juice from the lemon skeletons. Whisk in the olive oil and stir in the segments and any more juice. Stir in the parsley and season.

Lift the salmon out of the oil and gently turn it over, peel off the skin and scrape away the grey layer from under the skin. Serve with the salsa and salad.

Per serving 541 kcals, **protein** 34.7g, **carbohydrate** 3g, **fat** 43.1g, **saturated fat** 6.7g, **fibre** 0.9g, **salt** 0.8g

Smoked haddock rarebit with spinach

20 minutes | serves 2 | easy

2 fillets smoked haddock
200g spinach
knob of butter
100g mature Cheddar,
   grated
1 tsp wholegrain mustard
dash of Worcestershire
   sauce
1 egg
salt and freshly ground
   black pepper

This recipe for smoked haddock rarebit with spinach is really easy to make and ready in just 20 minutes – perfect for a midweek meal. The cheese topping makes it feel really special with minimal effort.

Poach the fillets of haddock in a pan of simmering water for 5 minutes. Drain, remove any skin and pat dry with kitchen paper.

Wilt the spinach in the same pan with the butter and season. Mix the cheese, mustard, Worcestershire sauce and egg in a bowl.

Divide the spinach between 2 heatproof dishes, leaving any excess liquid in the pan. Sit the haddock on top and spread over the rarebit mix. Grill until golden and bubbling.

Per serving 501 kcals, **protein** 46.8g, **carbohydrate** 3.5g, **fat** 32.7g, **saturated fat** 18.6g, **fibre** 3.1g, **salt** 4.5g

Puddings

Iced clementine possets with shortbread

15 minutes, plus freezing | serves 8 | easy

900g good-quality vanilla
   ice cream, just softened
200ml crème fraîche
grated zest and juice
   of 2 clementines
   or satsumas
grated zest and juice of
   1 grapefruit
300g lemon curd
shredded candied orange
   zest, to serve
shortbread, to serve

A somewhat lighter dessert that would also make a great pudding canapé. Plus they're stress-free as you can make them two or three days in advance.

Scrape the softened ice cream into a big mixing bowl with the crème fraîche, clementine and grapefruit zests and juice and the lemon curd. Mix until smooth – a big balloon whisk or spatula is good for this – then divide between 8 small freezerproof glasses. Freeze for at least 5 hours, or up to a week, and cover them in cling film once solid.

About 30 minutes before serving, remove from the freezer to soften a little. Serve with candied orange zest and shortbread.

Per serving 405 kcals, **protein** 4.7g, **carbohydrate** 45g, **fat** 22.9g, **saturated fat** 14.2g, **fibre** 0g, **salt** 0.2g

Self-saucing chocolate pudding

1 hour 15 minutes, plus overnight chilling | serves 8 | easy

40g butter, melted,
  plus extra for greasing
125g plain flour
2 tsp baking powder
2 tsp cocoa powder
60g golden caster sugar
120ml whole milk
1 egg
couple of drops
  vanilla extract
60g walnuts, chopped
  (optional)
cream or ice cream,
  to serve
salt

For the topping
180g muscovado sugar
2 tbsp cocoa powder

This chocolate pudding creates its own sauce below the sponge in the base of the dish. Perfect for entertaining, you can make it up in advance, then sprinkle sugar and cocoa on top and pour over some boiling water to cook it while you eat your main.

Butter a 1-litre baking dish. Sift the flour, baking powder and cocoa into a bowl and add the sugar and a pinch of salt.

Combine the milk, melted butter, egg and vanilla. Mix the two sets of ingredients together and add the nuts, if using. Pour the mixture into the baking dish. Cover with cling film and put in the fridge for 4–5 hours or overnight to set.

When you are ready to cook, remove the cling film and heat the oven to 180°C/Fan 160°C/Gas 4. Sprinkle the muscovado sugar and the cocoa over the pudding and pour 250ml of boiling water over the top. Put in the oven and cook for 45 minutes until puffy and firm in the centre – there will be a puddle of chocolate sauce in the base of the dish when you break the crust.

Serve with cream or ice cream.

Per serving 294 kcals, **protein** 4.2g, **carbohydrate** 45.5g, **fat** 11.8g, **saturated fat** 4.1g, **fibre** 1g, **salt** 0.44g

Spiced rhubarb crumble

45 minutes | serves 6 | easy

400g rhubarb, cut into
   short lengths
pinch of ground star anise
pinch of ground ginger
150g golden caster sugar
grated zest of 1 orange
fresh custard, to serve

For the crumble
150g plain flour
150g unsalted butter
100g porridge oats
150g demerara sugar
pinch of ground cinnamon

A classic crumble is the easiest of puddings to make and perfect for making use of seasonal fruit. This winter crumble is filled with sweet, tangy rhubarb and warming spices.

Preheat the oven to 180°C/Fan 160°C/Gas 4. Put the rhubarb, spices, sugar and orange zest in a pan and cook gently until just soft. Cool slightly, then spoon into a baking dish.

Rub the flour and butter together in a bowl to the consistency of breadcrumbs, stir in the oats and sugar, then spoon loosely but evenly on top of the fruit.

Bake for 20–30 minutes or until the top is crisp and golden. Serve with lashings of custard.

Per serving 537 kcals, **protein** 6.1g, **carbohydrate** 83.6g, **fat** 22.1g, **saturated fat** 13.3g, **fibre** 3.5g, **salt** 0.4g

Pear and chocolate puddings

1 hour | serves 6 | easy

100g unsalted butter, plus
  a little for greasing
160g light
  muscovado sugar
3 eggs
60g plain flour
30g cocoa powder
2 tsp baking powder
55g ground almonds
60ml whole milk
6 small, very ripe pears
pouring cream, to serve

The best chocolate puddings are the ones you don't have to share. We love these individual little pots of chocolate sponge and pear. Just add cream to serve and let your family and friends dive in.

Preheat the oven to 180°C/Fan 160°C/Gas 4. Butter 6 x 250ml ramekins. Beat the butter, sugar, eggs, flour, cocoa, baking powder, ground almonds and milk together.

Peel the pears and cut off the bottoms so that they will stand with a decent amount of height above the rims of the ramekins. Chop these bottom parts and fold them into the chocolate mixture. Divide the mixture between the ramekins until they are two-thirds full, then push in the tops of the pears. Bake for 30 minutes or until the pudding mix is puffed up around the pears. Serve with cream.

Per serving 433 kcals, **protein** 8.5g, **carbohydrate** 45.7g, **fat** 23.1g, **saturated fat** 10.6g, **fibre** 4.2g, **salt** 0.9g

Cardamom rice pudding

2 hours | serves 4 | easy

150g pudding rice
10 cardamom pods,
   lightly crushed
50g golden caster sugar
1 litre whole milk
20g butter, plus extra
   for greasing
jam or lightly poached
   apples, to serve

Everyone loves creamy baked rice pudding and it makes a great dessert to serve up for the family after Sunday lunch. This version uses fragrant cardamom for a subtle spiced finish.

Preheat the oven to 150°C/Fan 130°C/Gas 2. Lightly butter a 1.5-litre ovenproof dish. Toss the rice, cardamom pods and sugar into the dish. Stir in the milk, dot with butter and put in the oven. Cook for 30 minutes, then stir the rice and return to the oven for a further 30 minutes before stirring again. Return to the oven for a final hour without stirring. By this time the rice should be tender and creamy.

Serve the rice pudding hot with jam or lightly poached apples.

Per serving 385 kcals, **protein** 11.5g, **carbohydrate** 52.9g, **fat** 15.5g, **saturated fat** 9.4g, **fibre** 0g, **salt** 0.38g

Summer pudding

30 minutes, plus chilling | serves 6 | tricky but worth it

flavourless oil, for greasing
100g blackcurrants,
 stalks removed
100g redcurrants,
 stalks removed
100–150g golden caster
 sugar
500g raspberries
8–10 slices good-quality
 white sliced bread
double cream, to serve

This pudding is similar to a chocolate-filled cake but uses a mixture of summer fruits instead.

Oil 6 metal or plastic individual pudding basins and line them with cling film, leaving some overlapping (the oil helps the cling film to stick).

Put all the currants in a pan with the sugar and let them cook gently for 4–5 minutes until the fruit has given up a lot of juice. Stir in the raspberries to combine then tip the fruit into a sieve set over a bowl – keep the juice.

Use a biscuit cutter to cut circles from the bread to fit the top and bottom of the basins. Cut strips from the rest of the bread to fit the sides of the basins.

Dip the bread in the reserved juice and line the basins with them, juice side out (you can overlap a tiny bit). Spoon in the fruit along with some of the juice until the basins are full. Dip the top bread circles in the juice and press them gently into the top of the fruit. Keep any leftover juice. Fold over the excess cling film and press down gently.

Put the puddings on a tray then put a heavy board on top (weigh it down with tins if you like). Chill the puddings and the leftover juice overnight. The next day, carefully turn them out onto serving plates and remove the cling film.

Spoon over the reserved juice so the bread is soaked. Serve with double cream.

Per serving 189 kcals, **protein** 4.1g, **carbohydrate** 40.9g, **fat** 1.3g, **saturated fat** 0.2g, **fibre** 5.2g, **salt** 0.4g

Quince baked in honey and vanilla

3 hours, plus cooling | serves 6 | easy

200ml clear honey
   (use a flower honey
   for more flavour)
2 star anise
3 cinnamon sticks
2 vanilla pods, split
300ml water
3 quinces
Greek yoghurt, to serve

Quinces are in season from September through to December so this dish makes a lovely autumn or winter pudding. Serve with a side of Greek yoghurt.

Preheat the oven to 170°C/Fan 150°C/Gas 3. Add the honey, star anise, cinnamon and vanilla to the water. Quarter, peel and core the quinces and put each quarter straight into the honey mixture before it turns brown, turning them over so they are covered. Tip into a baking dish. Cover with foil and cook in the oven for 1½ hours, turning the quince halfway through.

Take off the foil – the quince should be tender by now and have turned redder and the syrup should be thicker. If the fruit is not completely tender, cook for another 30 minutes. When it is tender, take off the foil and cook it further if the syrup is not thick enough. Leave to cool in the syrup before serving with Greek yoghurt.

Per serving 124 kcals, **protein** 0.4g, **carbohydrate** 30.1g, **fat** 0.1g, **saturated fat** 0g, **fibre** 0.9g, **salt** 0g

Passion fruit puddle pudding

1 hour 10 minutes | serves 4 | easy

50g butter, softened, plus
   extra for greasing
200g golden caster sugar
6 passion fruit, insides
   scooped out, sift out
   the seeds if you prefer
juice of 2 lemons
3 eggs, separated
50g plain flour
250ml whole milk
cream or crème fraîche,
   to serve

Passion fruit self-saucing pudding, also known as passion fruit surprise pudding, is a great way to make passion fruit shine. You only need seven ingredients and an hour or so to make this beauty.

Preheat the oven to 180°C/Fan 160°C/Gas 4 and butter an ovenproof dish. Beat the butter and sugar together with electric beaters until pale. Add the passion fruit, lemon juice, egg yolks, flour and milk and stir with a wooden spoon until smooth.

Whisk the egg whites in a clean bowl until they hold soft peaks, then fold into the passion fruit mixture. Pour into the baking dish and set it in a baking tray half-filled with hot water. Bake for 45–50 minutes until the top is softly browned and set and the underneath is still like a sauce.

Serve hot with cream or crème fraîche.

Per serving 446 kcals, **protein** 8.7g, **carbohydrate** 64g, **fat** 16g, **saturated fat** 8.4g, **fibre** 3.4g, **salt** 0.4g

Eton mess

10 minutes | serves 6 | easy

350g strawberries,
    hulled and quartered,
    plus extra to decorate
4 meringue nests,
    broken into pieces
284ml carton double
    cream, lightly whipped

A classic English dessert that makes the most out of succulent, sweet British strawberries when they are in season. Strawberries, meringues and cream make a heavenly combination. Use ready-made meringues to make this dessert really simple.

Crush half of the strawberries to a rough pulp with the back of a fork or in a food processor.

Tip the meringues into a large bowl and stir in the cream. Add the strawberry pulp and strawberry quarters and gently fold everything together so you have ripples of pink through the white. Serve in glasses and decorate with extra strawberries.

Per serving 430 kcals, **protein** 2.4g, **carbohydrate** 20.4g, **fat** 38.2g, **saturated fat** 21.4g, **fibre** 1g, **salt** 0.09g

Fig tartes tatins

45 minutes | serves 4 | tricky but worth it

500g block puff pastry
plain flour, for dusting
200g golden caster sugar
80g unsalted butter
4 star anise
10-12 figs, halved
crème fraîche or ice cream,
  to serve

These tarts are very impressive and taste delicious. Smaller tarts are easier to turn out than one big one, but you can make just one to save time if you prefer.

Roll out the puff pastry on a floured surface to about 20p thickness. Put a round plate – about 12cm – on top and cut round it with a sharp knife to make 4 pastry circles, or cut out one large (12cm) tart base. Sprinkle with a little of the sugar and put them in the fridge.

Preheat the oven to 220°C/Fan 200°C/Gas 7. Put the remaining sugar and butter in a pan. Bring to the boil slowly, but do not stir it. When it begins to go a dark amber colour, add the star anise and cook for 1 minute more, then remove from the heat and pour into the bottom of 4 blini pans, approximately 12cm wide, or 4 small tart tins without loose bases. Make sure there is 1 star anise in each. If you're making one tart, pour into a 12cm cake tin. Put the figs in with the stem pointing towards the centre to make a wheel pattern. Put the pastry lid on the top and tuck the pastry in as though you were tucking in some bedsheets.

Put on a baking sheet and cook in the oven for 15–20 minutes, or until the pastry is golden, puffed and cooked through.

Take out of the oven and leave for a couple of minutes then turn onto warm plates. Serve with crème fraîche or ice cream.

Per serving 859 kcals, **protein** 8.7g, **carbohydrate** 101.7g, **fat** 46.1g, **saturated fat** 24.5g, **fibre** 2.1g, **salt** 1.3g

Index

Photography credits

MEAT-FREE
Fiery chickpea and harissa soup SAM STOWELL
Tortellini in a pea broth MYLES NEW
Cauliflower and cannellini bean soup ROGER STOWELL
Thai carrot and lemongrass soup SAM STOWELL
Smoky sweet potato soup TONY BRISCOE
Spring soup PHILIP WEBB
Tuscan bean and barley stew GARETH MORGANS
Creamed corn with chilli and smoky paprika STUART OVENDEN
Baked mushroom, potato and cheese hash SAM STOWELL
Spring onion and roasted red pepper frittata SAM STOWELL
Roast new potatoes with taleggio and capers GARETH MORGANS
Little gem lettuce and parm risotto PHILIP WEBB
Roasted roots and goat's cheese ADRIAN LAWRENCE
Pesto, pea and bean risotto GARETH MORGANS
Chickpea and tomato tagine JEAN CAZALS
Bombay egg and potato curry ANT DUNCAN
Tomato and onion bake GARETH MORGANS
Cauliflower, fennel and herb risotto DAVID MUNNS
Steakhouse-style spinach gratin GARETH MORGANS
Pan haggerty GARETH MORGANS
Winter greens and ricotta cannelloni MIKE ENGLISH

CHICKEN, POULTRY AND GAME
Smoky chicken and bean stew LIS PARSONS
Middle Eastern chicken and apricot stew MAJA SMEND
Chicken laksa ADRIAN LAWRENCE
Red pepper salad with baked chicken PHILIP WEBB
Roast chicken and Jerusalem artichokes MOWIE KAY
Barley risotto with chicken, beans & kale LARA HOLMES
Very quick chicken casserole SIMON WALTON
Thai butternut and chicken red curry GARETH MORGANS
Chicken jalfrezi MYLES NEW
Poule au pot PHILIP WEBB
Rosemary salt roast chicken GARETH MORGANS
Sunday chicken ANT DUNCAN
Turkey chilli bean stew SAM STOWELL
Roast cardamom and chilli butter-basted guinea fowl PHILIP WEBB
Braised rabbit with prunes and white wine MOWIE KAY
Gamekeeper's pie KRIS KIRKHAM

PORK, LAMB AND BEEF
Pea and coriander soup with chorizo SAM STOWELL
Vermicelli meatball soup DAVID MUNNS
Baked eggs with ratatouille and chorizo ADRIAN LAWRENCE
Storecupboard fried rice SAM STOWELL
Slow-cooked pork carnitas with tomatillo salsa ANT DUNCAN
Sticky pork and mangetout stir-fry SAM STOWELL
Gammon with leeks JEAN CAZALS
Radicchio and pancetta risotto ADRIAN LAWRENCE
Spelt risotto with pancetta and peas DAVID MUNNS
Pasta with crisp chorizo olive oil and parsley SAM STOWELL
Smoked ham hock and barley risotto primavera GARETH MORGANS
Pork with turnips PHILIP WEBB
Sausages with sage and butternut SAM STOWELL
Smoky baked pork and beans SAM STOWELL
Pinto bean and spicy sausage chilli GARETH MORGANS

Slow-roast pork with chilli and orange PHILIP WEBB
Chickpea and merguez stew with chilli garlic oil GARETH MORGANS
Sausage, beetroot and red cabbage hotpot ADRIAN LAWRENCE
Lamb kofta in sweet-sour tomato sauce PHILIP WEBB
Creamy lamb and tomato curry STUART OVENDEN
Meatballs with tomato and green olive DEBBIE TRELOAR
Peppers baked with lamb and rice STEVE JOHNSTON
Lamb rogan josh STUART OVENDEN
Lamb hotpot with swede topping PHILIP WEBB
Simple Persian-style lamb stew SAM STOWELL
Irish stew PETER CASSIDY
Slow-cooked lamb with spring veg and fresh mint sauce GARETH MORGANS
Leg of lamb with pomegranate and balsamic onions ANT DUNCAN
Slow-braised lamb shanks with coconut and cardamom SAM STOWELL
Mustard mac 'n' cheese with pastrami & crumbs SAM STOWELL
Chilli con carne LARA HOLMES
Diner-style chilli SAM STOWELL
10-minute beef stroganoff SAM STOWELL
Beef paprikash MAJA SMEND
Slow-braised Korean short ribs PETER CASSIDY
Vietnamese beef and lemongrass SAM STOWELL
Beef, red wine and black olive stew GARETH MORGANS
Tuscan slow-cooked shin of beef with Chianti ANT DUNCAN
Cantonese braised turnips with short ribs GARETH MORGANS
Rib of beef roasted over potatoes PHILIP WEBB

FISH AND SEAFOOD
Corn, chive and prawn chowder BRETT STEVENS
Cheat's seafood stew LARA HOLMES
Mussel and tomato chowder PHILIP WEBB
Spicy crab and sweetcorn chowder with avocado GARETH MORGAN
Fish curry with tomatoes and tamarind SAM STOWELL
Spanish prawns, peppers and aioli ANT DUNCAN
Linguine with samphire and prawns PHILIP WEBB
Saffron mussels with orzo & tomatoes MIKE ENGLISH
Jansson's temptation GUS FILGATE
Prawn and dill pilaf DAVID MUNNS
Spanish rice with saffron and mussels GARETH MORGANS
Tuna, sweet potato and gruyère melt MIKE ENGLISH
Confit salmon with lemon and parsley salsa ANT DUNCAN
Smoked haddock rarebit with spinach STUART OVENDEN

PUDDINGS
Iced clementine possets with shortbread ANT DUNCAN
Self-saucing chocolate pudding GARETH MORGANS
Spiced rhubarb crumble MYLES NEW
Pear and chocolate puddings STUART OVENDEN
Cardamom rice pudding BRETT STEVENS
Summer pudding GARETH MORGANS
Quince baked in honey and vanilla PHILIP WEBB
Passion fruit puddle pudding GARETH MORGANS
Eton mess MYLES NEW
Fig tartes tatins GARETH MORGANS